Beyond the Coffee Shop

Riding 1970s Moto Guzzis in Northern Canada

Nick Adams

Copyright © 2015 Nick Adams

All rights reserved.

ISBN-13: 978-1515311584

ISBN-10: 1515311589

CONTENTS

Foreword

The Happy Place	5
Beginnings	6
The Middle Years	11
Getting to Know You	11
Getting to Know All About You	20
Stolen Days	23
The Trans-Labrador Highway	33
A New Bike	48
Highway 138 to Natashquan	53
James Bay Road Debacle	65
....And I Only Saw 3 Bears	73
To See a Panther	79
Yet Another Bike	84
The Swisha Road	87
Return to the Trans-Taiga	94
Final Thoughts	104
Maps	105

FOREWORD

If you are looking for high adventure, outrageous acts of courage or 'first person to...............'(fill in the blank yourself), you had best look elsewhere. These are simple road tales, mini trips, extended weekend or week long jaunts by an oldish guy riding a bunch of oldish Moto Guzzis.

Over last few years I have written a number of short, photo-illustrated descriptions of my various motorcycle adventures and published them to active motorcycle forums - mainly the 'Wildguzzi Forum and Adventure Rider Forum. These trip reports were written as disconnected postings, usually interspersed with comments and observations by other forum inhabitants.

My normal modus operandi - one which has been a source of immense frustration to my long suffering wife, is to get on the computer as soon as I get home, sometimes even before eating or hitting the bathtub, and start cranking out my story while it is still fresh in my mind. A four day trip spills over into five as I struggle to find the words, organize the photographs and sometimes compile a very amateurish video version to post on Youtube.

Some of the other materials contained in this mish-mash are segments, paragraphs, bits and pieces and adaptations of short articles that have either been pasted up on my web site or have been published in that most excellent of classic bike magazines 'RealClassic'. So, if some of the material contained herein feels startlingly familiar, you only have yourself to blame for spending too much time reading motorcycling adventures on line or motorcycle magazines when you should be working or paying attention to your loved ones. Guess how I know about that!

THE HAPPY PLACE

You know how it goes. You're sitting in the big, leather chair and the dentist says, *"You'll feel a little squeeze"* as he skewers the roof of your mouth to your eyeball. It's about then I start searching for my Happy Place - the place I can call up in my memory where there the dentist drilling holes in my head dissolves into the background, and peace and tranquility settle all around.

During a series of visits for a cluster of fillings, I used to head off to a small island in the English River in remote northwestern Ontario. My friend Steve and I had camped there once as dusk was falling. As the light began to fail, the wind dropped and it became remarkably still, the silence broken only by the sound of the wing beats of rafts of small ducks flying overhead from the bay opposite. A little later, three moose swam across from the mainland to the adjacent island, the sound of their breath carrying on the still air.

I found it easy to dive back there in my mind: the sights, sounds and smells were so firmly embedded, and usually by the time I had got to the part where the beaver was swimming around the island, verbally chastising my dog, the drilling was done and it was time to emerge back in to the present.

Fast forward a few years and I'm back in the dentists chair, this time for a root canal to fix a toothache that had plagued me throughout a motorcycle trip across Labrador. As the needle went in and the drilling started, I found myself heading for a new location and a new set of memories. This time, I was rolling along an isolated, unpaved road. Quiet had been replaced by the steady beat of a Guzzi V-twin, the mellow drone of the exhaust and the sound of tyres on loose gravel. I could feel the wind on my face, the sun on my skin, the comforting vibration through the handlebars and the seat. That uniquely boreal forest smell of balsam and strawberries, mixed with gravel dust was in my nostrils. There was no traffic, nobody for miles, just an endless road, snaking through the forest and the pulsing of the engine.

Dentist? What dentist - I was in my new Happy Place.

BEGINNINGS

"Mum, can I get a motorbike?"

"You are never bringing a motorbike to this house!"

"OK Mum".

In the UK, from the age of sixteen you used to be able to ride any two wheeled vehicle under 250cc's on 'L' plates as a learner rider. As far as my mum was concerned, full sized motorbikes were the spawn of the devil and would never to be allowed at our home. Smaller bikes and scooters, for some irrational reason, were grudgingly permissible. My Dad? He just kept quiet.

Despite Mum's antipathy, my teenage years were filled with motorized two-wheelers. I have a grainy picture of my brother Tim and me sitting on his Lambretta GT200 from long before I ever had a bike of my own. I'm all teeth and cheeks, while Tim, the impossibly cool, older brother, looks like a slim, white version of James Brown. I don't think he ever actually deigned to take me for a ride on that scooter (and my mother certainly wouldn't have allowed it) but the hook had been dangled and set.

Almost as soon as I turned 16, I was able to pry his other bike from him with the proceeds from my morning paper round. It was a worn out Lambretta D150, one of the early D's with no body panels to speak of, a three speed gearbox and a clutch like a light switch. I must have stalled that thing about forty times before I finally got the hang of the relationship between the clutch and the throttle and was able to weave my way from our driveway and out on to the public roads. Even now, almost fifty years later, I can still remember
riding one of the high, open roads across the top of the Cotswolds, the two stroke motor humming away beneath me, the wind in my face and the view stretching out for miles in all directions. Speed wasn't important to me, which was probably a good thing because I think flat out that 'D' was only good for about 45mph, but it introduced me to the world of powered two-wheeled transportation and the exotic dream that with a little fuel in the tank, you could head for the horizon.

I have no idea what happened to the 'D'. From time to time it would soft-seize, so perhaps it finally locked up for good. It's more likely though, that it was swapped for some other bottom of the barrel bike, as I had a whole succession of small scooters in those early days, two of which I remember with particular fondness. My Lambretta Li 125 is lodged in my memory as the bike least likely to get me home. It would start and run well; well enough at least to get me most of the way to where I wanted to be, before spluttering to a stop at the side of the road. I pushed that bike countless miles and never did manage to cure its intransigence. The second memorable scooter - a Triumph Tigress - with its 250cc, twin cylinder ,4 stroke engine promised massive power and speed but only managed to provide endless disappointment. I never really got the Tigress running for long enough to accumulate any miles and before long, it was traded for some other clunker. Gradually the scooters were replaced by small motorbikes. My first, a BSA C15, was allowed a place in the parental garage since it was my only way to get to and from my job in the production control office at the ailing BSA factory in Small Heath and it was a 'small' bike. Although C15s have a reputation for being fragile, mine behaved flawlessly, never failing to start and always getting me where I wanted to go. But as reliable and useful as the C15 continued to be, my mind had already been drifting towards larger and more powerful bikes.

I took my riding test on the BSA in the pouring rain. In those days you just rode around a predetermined route while the examiner watched you from the side of the road. One of the key elements of the test was the 'emergency stop'. The examiner would step out into the road holding his clipboard and your job was to come to a quick, controlled stop without falling off or ploughing into him. When I saw him step out in front of me, I braked hard, but my rear wheel slid out sideways on the wet, greasy, diesel soaked road. I stopped with inches to spare with the rear wheel almost level with the front. I was sure I must have failed the test, but instead of being upset, the examiner passed me my ticket and congratulated me on managing to keep the bike under control in difficult circumstances.

Now I could legally ride any size motorbike.

"Mum, I just passed my motorbike test".

"You are never bringing a motorbike to this house!"

I had anticipated this. Unbeknownst to my parents, I already had a 'big' motorbike. A few weeks earlier I had bought a 600cc 1950 Panther Redwing 100 from a former girlfriend's brother for the princely sum of 10 pounds, had rented a small lock-up garage and had secretly been working on it while my parents thought I was out hanging around with friends. When I bought it, it was in original condition. All the tinware was in place, and everything worked as it should. I can even remember the licence plate number - PTW 116, if anyone knows of its whereabouts.

Even through my rose-tinted bifocals I'll admit it was a bit of a beast. It had square tyres from an earlier life hauling a sidecar, which made its inherently precarious handling verge on the mutinous. It shook, it roared, it often stalled, and it tried its best to break my ankle whenever I got lazy and didn't adjust the advance/retard just so, before trying to kick it into life. But I loved it. I loved the lazy loping way its long-stroke engine pulled like an express, no matter which gear you were in. I loved the look of that massive, black, sloping iron cylinder, reaching towards the headstock from what seemed like a single block of aluminum at the bottom end. And I adored the gratuitously fat, double exhaust pipes emerging from its twin-port head. Most of all, being sixteen remember, I loved the way you could make it bark and backfire by suddenly retarding the ignition.

My friend John and I butchered it. We stripped off everything we considered old fashioned or unnecessary, including the toolbox and the original steel mudguards, bolted on a dual seat and a home-made sissy bar, then headed up the M6 to Scotland. I told my parents that we were going to Scotland: I certainly didn't tell them how!

The ride up was our first taste of adventure. Inevitably, it was pouring rain and we were inadequately dressed. The Panther would cruise at 60mph: almost exactly the same speed as the heavy goods vehicles. We could edge past them on the uphill sections, the spray from their massive wheels drenching us, our black PVC rain coats flapping wildly in the wind, then they would roar past us on the downhills, the wind blast sucking us into the soaking vortex in their wake. Were we having fun? You bet!

The primary chain broke just south of Glasgow, but a friendly - or perhaps sympathetic - farmer allowed us to leave the bike in his yard while we hitch-hiked to the nearest bike shop to find a replacement. Fortunately primary chains for old British singles were standard sizes, so finding a replacement was easy. Our tent poles vibrated off somewhere on the road between Dumfries and Kilmarnock, only to be replaced, for free, by a generous manager at Blacks of Greenock. Although it was Saturday morning and there was no-one else around, he took pity on two bedraggled bikers, took us in to the closed-up factory and fitted our tent with a new set of poles. It wasn't even a Blacks tent.

Beyond Glasgow, both the weather and the scenery improved and the bike hauled the two of us and our gear flawlessly up and down the west coast of the Highlands for almost two weeks. At one point we came across two girls struggling to walk the last few miles to a youth hostel.

Like good knight's errant, while John stayed and socialized with one of the girls, I ferried the other to the hostel then returned for the second. Although neither girl had ever ridden on a motorbike before, the first matched my body language perfectly and being lighter than John, it was as if she wasn't there. The second girl fought to stay upright and made negotiating the tighter corners on those square tyres quite a battle.

Eventually our spell of good luck broke. It started to rain so we headed for home. After a few miles the Panther spluttered, then died completely. Water in the magneto was beyond my limited capacity to fix, even if I had the knowledge or skill to diagnose it. All I knew was that we were stranded at the side of a busy highway, soaked through and cold, with a bike I couldn't even get to fire, no matter how many times I jumped on the kickstart. John and I did what seemed logical at the time - we unbolted the tax disk, abandoned the Panther and hitch-hiked home.

Two weeks later my mother handed me the phone. In a strong Scottish accent, the policeman at the other end curtly advised me that they had my Panther at the police station (I can no longer remember which one - but it was a small town just north of Edinburgh) and that I was to collect it forthwith.

To say that my mother was angry and disappointed would be an understatement, but being an inherently practical person, she accepted the reality of the situation and loaned me the money for the train fare north. Two days later, I sheepishly told the desk sergeant that I had arrived to collect my bike. With barely a word he led me out back to a shed and there was my bike, dirty, dry, but otherwise very much as we had left it. I had no idea what to do next or what kind of trouble I was in, so I turned on the fuel, adjusted the choke and advance/retard, lifted the decompression lever with my toe, worked the piston past top-dead-centre, then gave it a kick. To my astonishment, it bellowed into life as if nothing had ever been the matter.

Back inside, I told the desk sergeant that I had managed to get the bike running.

"Right - off you go then", he said dismissively.

There was no mention of charges for abandoning the bike or a bill for hauling it in from where we had left it. He didn't even ask to see my licence, tax disk or insurance. I rode away nervous, but grateful.

Three of the most memorable events of that trip occurred because the bike we were riding was old and a bit unreliable. In the decades that have past since, the rest of the trip has long ago blended in to a vague memory of lochs and mountains, no longer distinguishable from a host of other Scotland holidays. But I will forever remember the helpfulness of the farmer and the Blacks manager, and perhaps most of all, the gruff kindness and understanding shown by the police.

Since then, I have come to understand that this first foray into the world of motorcycle touring had a profound influence on what I do now, how I do it and how it gives me pleasure. I learned that there is real value to riding older, sometimes unreliable machinery. It doesn't matter if the bike breaks down or the weather is foul. Somehow, it will all turn out all right. Most of all though, it exposes you to a world where other people have an opportunity to show you their best, and that is what lasting memories are made of.

Nick and Tim, about 1965

THE MIDDLE YEARS

I would love to be able to tell you that I had an unbroken string of increasingly desirable motorbikes which I rode all over the globe, culminating in my current crop of Moto Guzzis, but it simply wouldn't be true. The desire to be warm and dry erupted from time to time, so my early motorbike history is liberally sprinkled with a succession of clunky three-wheelers and cars. The 1950 Panther disappeared, eventually replaced with a 1964 650 Panther 120. The later model never worked its way into my heart as the first one had and was soon gone. An Ariel Leader and other bikes came and went, then, after a disastrous and expensive dalliance with a couple of Reliant three-wheelers, another BSA came into my life.

My BSA Royal Star 500 turned out to be a great bike. It was smooth (for a British twin), fast enough (for a British twin) and reliable enough (for a British twin). At the time, I was living and working in Norfolk and the BSA was used for regular weekend commutes back to the Birmingham area to visit my recently widowed mother, a task it performed without a single hiccup.

Dad had died of a heart attack at the age of 51, but some years before that, he had guiltily admitted a fondness for motorbikes. As my brothers and I were growing up, he had never talked about his involvement in the war: the memories of his dozens of bombing raids over Germany in Halifaxs and Ansons was far too painful, but he did admit to having had a terrific time in Japan, mostly because of the opportunities to ride the Matchless 'pool' bikes on a regular basis. I hadn't realised it, but I'd had an ally all along.

The BSA remained trouble free until I needed it most. I had met a Canadian girl and had promised to take her on a tour around Scotland on the bike, just as the main bearings were starting to become intrusively noisy. There was no way I could chance a long, two-up trip with failing bearings, so I did the only thing I could do - I disassembled the engine on the living room floor, sourced replacement bearings and rebuilt the engine just in time. I had never done anything even remotely that mechanically adventurous before, but by closely following the repair manual to the letter, I was able to complete the job. To my delight and surprise, the thing actually ran afterwards. That BSA carried us without complaint all the way up the west coast of Scotland, across to the Orkneys and back home again.

Eventually the girlfriend disappeared back to Canada and I was left with a dilemma: did I sell the bike and fly over to visit, with who knows what future that might bring, or did I trade the BSA in against the brand new Norton Interstate 850 that I had been eyeing in the local motorcycle shop. In the end passion won out over.................. passion. I spent that Christmas with the girlfriend's family, then returned to Canada the following March for a longer stay. Little did I know how much longer that would be. During my second trip to Canada, I had cast around a little to see whether there were any work opportunities in Canadian archaeology. I had been working in British archaeology for quite a few years, so I thought some, at least, of my experience and knowledge must be transferable, even if the specifics were different. I managed to get myself a few interviews, including one with the guy that was head of the Ontario government's archaeology program. To cut a fairly lengthy and involved story short, on the very day my return flight left for the UK, I was on a Greyhound bus heading north to Sault Ste. Marie to take up my position as a field archaeologist for northeastern Ontario. Over the next few years, a work visa eventually morphed into landed immigrant status, which, many years later, morphed into full citizenship. Thirty-eight years later, I'm still here!

In Canada, bikes are positively seasonal. Once I saw my first winter, it dispelled any thoughts that riding all year round was a viable proposition. Instead of being transportation, motorbikes are toys. All I saw on the roads were posturing oafs on Harleys and that didn't appeal to me at all. My motorcycle addiction was put on the back burner, and the burner was off.

It's a familiar story. The relationship with the girlfriend fizzled out. A new relationship developed, followed by marriage and after a few years, kids - three of the blighters.

Over the years the motorcycling urge raised its ugly head from time to time but never really caught my full attention. A Norton Atlas lingered around our house briefly, never ran properly and soon departed. A few years later, a dreadful Kawasaki 454 LTD fell into my lap. That thing was so ugly and uncomfortable that I could barely stand to look at it. It had low oil pressure, was in serious need of some engine work, and was soon gone. More years went by. If I thought about bikes at all, it was with that misty eyed fondness that is reserved for things past.

Then Doug turned up.

There are many names for Doug, none of which can be repeated here. He is one of those larger than life characters who cuts a swath through the world with his unique, often outrageous personality. He'd joined my merry band of indigent workers a few years back. Against all my expectations had turned out to be an efficient, skilled and reliable employee and had quickly become a friend.

One day he arrived at my house on a Honda CB350 and insisted that I take it for a ride. I just rode it up the street. I went up through the gears and back down through the gears and long before I turned back into my driveway, I was hooked all over again. I had to have another bike. We immediately started searching the on-line advertisements and within minutes had found a bike that spoke to me: a 1972 Moto Guzzi Eldorado for sale about 300 kilometres away. As a teenager I had always lusted after Moto Guzzis, but at that time they had seemed impossibly exotic and expensive (particularly the latter) and I had put them out of my mind.

Now, here in front of me, was a one owner bike with 56,000 kilometres on the clock. The troublesome chrome-lined cylinders (the chrome flakes off and destroys bearings) had already been replaced with factory new iron sleeved cylinders, upping displacement from the original 844cc to 949cc. It looked to be in relatively good condition. One quick phone call, a few minutes hitching up the trailer and we were on the road. A few hours later she was mine.

Doug

GETTING TO KNOW YOU...

Let's get all the cliches out of the way straight away. Motorcycle magazines are full of them. In fact, you can hardly read a moto-magazine article without the same old nonsense being trotted out, time after time.

Yes, the Moto Guzzi v-twins lurch slightly to the right on startup but it won't throw the bike off the stand if you twist the throttle. Yes, the cylinders are down by your knees, but no, even at 6' 2" my knees never hit them and don't get hot. Drive-shaft jacking may lift the rear of the bike slightly if you are a ham-fisted moron with no throttle control, but in the real world, it simply doesn't exist as an issue and is never noticeable. No, the tranverse V-twin isn't derived from a tractor motor, and although Moto Guzzi did once produce a peculiar three wheeled, three wheel drive tractor powered by a V-twin engine, the engines are unrelated, other than their basic layout.

Well that's enough of that drivel. Now I can tell you about my bike. The 1972 Moto Guzzi Eldorado is derived from the famous V700, much beloved by police forces in California and elsewhere for its tireless power and remarkable reliability. Mine had been sitting unused but regularly maintained since the mid-nineteen eighties. As soon as we got it home, Doug and I did some basic cleanup. We changed the oil, tore into the carbs and cleaned them within an inch of their lives, cleaned the points, replaced the plugs then started it up.

1972 Moto Guzzi Eldorado - from the ad.

The Eldorado has bags of character as I discovered on my first ride. You start it by turning the key in the middle of the dash, just like starting a car. There is no kickstart, but with a car-sized battery (mine is from a lawn tractor), starting is rarely a problem. With most bikes, the starter spins the engine quickly. On this bike though, the starter strains to turn against compression, before the engine bursts into life. It's disconcerting at first - you think the engine isn't going to turn over - but it always does.

The two Del Orto VHB29 carbs have individual choke levers, but you can flick them off almost immediately and the bike settles to a steady, even idle.

On some bikes the dry two plate clutch rattles in neutral although mine is quiet and the clutch action is light. Pull in the lever and press down on the left side heel and toe gear change with your heel. Ignore any grinding or clunking noises and the slight lurch forward as the gear is selected. Once it's in, it's in. You need a merest whiff of throttle to move off smoothly, the massive flywheel making it virtually impossible to stall. At low revs the engine is surprisingly grumbly, chugging forward in a series of pulses and only smoothing out once the revs rise over about 2500. Gear changes need to be leisurely, but the box is robust, each gear engaging securely with a slight clunk when you press down on the meaty lever. At 4000 rpm, which equates to about 65mph, the engine becomes positively silky. This is a speed the bike is happy to maintain all day, day after day.

At first the handling seems a little on the heavy side, but it is stable and predictable. You sit upright, with your feet directly below your thighs in a comfortable "standard" riding stance. It's all-day comfortable, as long as I remember my beaded and sheepskin seat covers. On long, fast, uneven bends the rear may wallow a bit, but it never feels disconcerting or worrisome.

As for the brakes, obviously they can't compare with modern stoppers and were even considered a bit weak by the contemporary motorcycle press. After sailing right through a couple of intersections when the lights changed unexpectedly, with the brakes fully on, and little happening, I exchanged the original 2 leading shoe front brake for a 4 leading shoe brake from a 1974 Guzzi California I bought as a parts bike. It's a vast improvement. At first it feels as though not much is happening, but squeeze a little harder, the nose dips, you start to feel the force on your arms and there is a real danger of locking up the front wheel. Not for me the ghastly grafting of disk brakes and forks from a later model, with all the aesthetic compromises that entails. Incidentally, that California ended up being too good just to raid for parts, so I put the 2 leading shoe brake on it and sold it to Doug after he holed a piston on his

CB350. It's now his daily rider, and as reliable as granite.

It didn't take me long before I started to trust the Eldorado. Turn the key - she starts. Head for the horizon - she will take you there.

Our first lengthy trip together was up the south shore of the St. Lawrence River to the Chic Choc mountains on the Gaspe peninsula. I had been watching the '*Lord of the Rings*', for the n'th time, when the part where Bilbo say's "*But I want to see mountains again Gandalf, mountains*", struck me in a way I couldn't shake.

I had spent much of my youth hiking in upland Britain. Those hilltops were scalped of their native forest back in the Neolithic. When the hills and mountains aren't covered in cloud (which is much of the time), the views go on for ever and it feels as though you are walking on the roof of the world - a perfect landscape for hiking. Transplanted to the endless forests and level topography of Ontario, I, like Bilbo, periodically ache for those open spaces.

I had read that the tops of the Chic-Choc mountains on Quebec's Gaspe Peninsula have an arctic environment and are well above the tree line. With their highest point reaching just over 4000 feet (1200m) they barely rate on the global scale as mountains, but they are exposed to the full force of winter winds whistling up the St. Lawrence valley which keeps their climate......well, bracing, and keeps their summits free of those pesky trees. It seemed like just the place for me.

By 11AM the next day, I was on my the Eldorado, heading east towards Quebec. Now its a curious thing about older bikes - you ride along (or at least I do), checking for unusual sounds, looking between your legs to see if you've sprung a leak, and generally fretting that some major part is going to let go in a frenzy of sparks and hot metal, so I started the journey fairly slowly, avoiding the main highways and sticking to the less high speed routes.

My route took me east along the south shore of the St. Lawrence, past Montreal and eventually on to the divided Highway 20 towards Quebec City. By that time I had given up fretting about the bike and begun to enjoy blasting along at whatever speed I felt like.

Of course, the bike loved it. It has a particular sweet spot that starts at about 120kph and extends - well, I never did find out - but it's certainly happy droning along with the modern traffic, at least 20kph above the posted speed.

I won't try to pretend that the journey there or back was trouble free. Somewhere between Quebec City and Riviere du Loup the old girl started to spit and sputter and when I pulled over to investigate, she stalled. Fuel was pouring from the base of the off-side carburetor. I quickly turned off the ignition, shut off the fuel tap and unleashed my tool kit. Older bikes in general, and older Moto Guzzis in particular are stone-age simple, so even with my rudimentary wrenching skills, I was able to tear the carburetor to pieces, clean the crud out of the offending jet, and reassemble it in a matter of minutes, so it came as a bit of a shock to see fuel pouring all over the crankcase as soon as I turned the tap again. Darn! In my rush to get rolling, I hadn't seated the rubber float bowl gasket properly. Fortunately, it was an easy fix, and within another five minutes I was on my way.

Quebec is great! Before heading to the Gaspesie Park camp ground at the base of the Chic Chocs, I filled up on all the necessities of life - local wine, fresh baguettes, varieties of cheese I'd never heard of, but which turned out to be wonderful anyway, a full tank of fuel and some 20/50 oil - all at the local gas station. This is quite a contrast to puritanical Ontario where the distribution of booze is strictly managed by the government, and where fresh food and gas stations are mutually exclusive. That night, fortified by a belly full of bread and cheese, comfortably washed down by the wine, I slept in my hammock like a baby.

Considering the previous evening, I was feeling surprisingly sprightly when I woke up at around 5 AM, the next day. I packed the bike as quietly as possible so as not to disturb my camping neighbours, then rode along a few kilometers of gravel road to the start of the hiking trail for Mount Richardson.

The first part of the trail consisted of a steady climb on a cobble trail through thick forest: certainly not what I had visualized or hoped for. Soon enough though, I emerged onto a ridge of stunted bushes and bare rock where I could finally see the top of Mount Richardson and the surrounding mountains poking through the valley mists. It was a stunning sight - well worth the slog through the dew laden forest. The top of Mount Richardson was still some distance away, but something moving along the skyline caught my eye. Two Caribou were silhouetted against the bright blue sky. I couldn't believe my good luck!

Reaching the summit was a bit of a scramble up a steep but well used path, with loose rock under foot. As the park literature had promised, the top few hundred feet of Mount Richardson were almost bald - just a few scraggly patches of lichen and moss filled the gaps between scree and bare rock.

I had the mountain to myself! I celebrated with a couple of granola bars and a few swigs of juice as I hunkered between the rocks to shelter from the cold wind that was blowing across the summit. To the north and west, the land fell steeply away, providing a magnificent view of Mount Albert and the rest of the Chic-Chocs disappearing into the misty distance. To the south and east.....what was that? Just over the skyline, but not more than thirty feet from where I was sitting, I could see what looked like a couple of sticks waving about. I hastily grabbed my camera and moved down the slope to investigate. To my delight, the sticks turned out to be the antlers of the two Caribou I had seen on the ridge earlier. They were lying peacefully in a small mossy hollow, chewing the cud, not ten feet below me. Once they saw me, they stumbled to their feet and ambled off down the slope, but not before I shot off a quick couple of pictures to keep them fresh in my memory.

By the time I was back down in the forest, the mist was disappearing from the valley and others were afoot on the trail - friendly folk - almost all of whom were Quebecois and who immediately engaged me in conversation with a blistering, and to me, totally incomprehensible outburst of French. My command of the French language extends to Vin Rouge, Fromage, and my favourite and only phrase which I use regardless of the situation: "*Je suis desole; Je ne parle pas le francais*", accompanied by a apologetic raising of the palms. Some of the hikers immediately switched to perfect English and the conversation proceeded: those who couldn't shrugged regretfully, and we would go our different ways. The problem was, for some reason, about every third time I met someone, I would happily blurt out: "*Je suis Desiree. Je ne parle pas le francais.*" No wonder I got some strange looks.

I spent the rest of the day riding to the south coast of the Gaspe Peninsula. The road follows the Cascapedia River for virtually the whole way as it winds through the mountains. The road is fairly well surfaced, with lots of sweeping turns. It is definitely one to add to your bucket list. From there I turned northeast again - this time up the Matapedia Valley, hitting the north shore again at Mont Joli. By this time I was exhausted, so I stopped at a motel just short of Rimouski where I spent the evening sitting on a plastic chair outside my room, guzzling another bottle of cheap Quebec wine and admiring my bike while the sun went down over the St. Lawrence. What a bike - built in 1972 and still going strong.

On the last leg of the trip - the long haul back towards Montreal - she developed a bit of an oil leak from tubing for my external oil filter. The previous owner had used rigid copper water pipe to literally plumb in an external oil filter and the soldered joints were starting to separate. It wasn't serious: just enough to keep my mind occupied. It leaked enough oil to make a bit of a mess of the engine and my right boot, but not enough to slow our journey.

On my return, I replaced the copper pipe with flexible hose, custom made by the local hydraulic supply shop. She also developed a worrisome low rev vibration. This turned out to be a broken generator mount - an old Guzzi weak spot - and one which was to reappear on a later trip with disastrous consequences. Generally though, she handled the ride with aplomb, carrying me safely and in style and comfort to an unexpected and magical rendezvous on top of Mount Richardson.

For the briefest time, I had my head up above the trees, breathed the fresh mountain air, and could see for miles. It will tide me over - until, like Bilbo, I have to see mountains again.

Caribou near the summit of Mount Richardson

GETTING TO KNOW ALL ABOUT YOU...

The Eldorado and I were becoming comfortable riding 500 mile days together. I quickly discovered that I really enjoy riding on remote roads, alone and started to look forward to any time I could sneak away from home and work for a few days. Some people like riding with others or travel by stopping and seeing all the sights along a route. Not me! Long hours alone in the saddle, accompanied by the wind, the passing scenery, and the sound and feel of the engine is my pleasure. I think of it as a kind of mobile meditation. It must be, because although I know my mind is busy during these trips, I've no idea where it goes. I do like to have a destination or a purpose in mind though and while I don't avoid or ignore the sights along the way and will even stop to take photographs, the riding is what excites me. I don't really like stopping at all. The necessity of buying fuel from time to time is an unfortunate necessity: the need for food is intrusive, the need to rest my backside is a pain.

Years of working in northern Ontario, conducting archaeological surveys by canoe, fed my passion for isolation. I developed a comfort in being in out-of-the-way places. Extending this to motorcycle travel was inevitable and easy.

One of things I found out fairly early on in our relationship was that the Eldorado was an extremely capable bike on gravel and dirt roads. With a low centre of gravity and predictable handling, she plugs along comfortably, always with torque and power in reserve when the going gets loose and squirrely. I began to search out long roads to isolated places to feed these passions. If they were unpaved, so much the better.

With only a few days at my disposal, I opted to explore the road from Baie Comeau north to Labrador City. Anyone who has ever looked at Google Earth images of Canada is likely to have noticed a rather unusual lake which lies half way between the St. Lawrence River and Labrador City. It is huge, almost 70 kilometers across and almost perfectly circular - occupying the impact crater from a massive meteorite strike about 215 million years ago. A Hydro Quebec dam at the southern end retains the water, which now surrounds a huge island, so that from space it looks like a gigantic 'O' ring. What could be better than a quick blast up the St. Lawrence valley, a left turn up Highway 389 to the dam at Manic-5, a quick look at the lake, another 300 kilometers of mostly unpaved, winding road up to Labrador City, the a rewind blast home? Just the very thing for an almost 40 year old motorcycle.

Astonishingly, the bike behaved flawlessly, the weather was perfect, there was virtually no other traffic, the scenery just rolled on and on, mile after mile of gorgeous tree clad hills, rocky outcrops, lakes, streams and rivers. The massive dam at Manic-5 is an awesome piece of engineering, but Lac Manicouagan was a bit of a disappointment. Don't get me wrong, it's a beautiful, scenic lake, surrounded by forested rocky hills - it's just that from the ground, you cannot get any sense of its enormous size or its unusual shape. It looks just like any other large, northern Canada lake.

In all, I covered about 3200 kilometers in four days. The only hiccup was the loss of a large bolt from the lower triple tree on the front forks, but a quick stop at an automotive parts place in Labrador City soon had the forks held on properly again (with an SAE, not metric nut and bolt), and me and the bike back in action. I had zero punctures, zero breakdowns and zero traffic issues. I didn't run out of fuel or oil. I didn't fall off and hurt myself. I didn't get lost or have to hold anything together with duct tape, zip ties or glue. The bike just rolled along at any speed I chose, happily keeping up with traffic on the highways: happily bouncing along through soft gravel and over lumpy rocks on the unpaved sections.

It was all too easy - where's the fun in that! I needed something a little more........testing.

Between Labrador City and Manic-5

Heading in to Labrador City

STOLEN DAYS

Canada is blessed with thousands of kilometers of empty roads which seem to wind on forever through forested hills and between still blue lakes. Between May and September, cruisers, full-dress two wheeled road yachts, street bikes, dual sports and crotch rockets ply these roads, as riders pack in as much road time as the seasons and road conditions will allow. Congestion simply isn't part of the landscape. It is motorcycle heaven.

Unfortunately for those of us that get their vehicular pleasure on two wheels, Canada also has winter. With the exception of the lucky folks who inhabit the coastal parts of British Columbia (disparagingly referred to as "Lotus Land" by those who live in the rest of the country), where it is possible to ride all year round if you don't mind getting wet, most sensible people hang up their leathers in October, push the bike into the garage, throw some fuel stabilizer in the gas tank, put the winter tires on the pickup truck and abandon all hope of riding again until April or May. Snow and ice covered roads and temperatures which stay well below freezing for weeks at a time, discourage all but the most foolhardy or suicidal from attempting to ride.

But I did say 'most'!

For some of us, waiting four or five months to ride again is too great a strain on our mental health. We watch the weather forecasts and constantly check the road condition reports, searching for those rare and magical days when the roads are bare and dry, the air temperature doesn't feel as though it needs to be measured in degrees Kelvin, and the skies are cloud free. These are the stolen days: the few days in each winter when it is possible to ride without landing on your ear before you reach the first corner and the danger of life threatening frostbite is minimal. They are as rare as hen's teeth, but when they arrive, its time to shovel the snow away from the garage door, wheel the bike into the bright sunshine, and see if the old girl will start.

Those first few turns of the starter cause grunting and spluttering as the gas reaches the carbs, and the crankshaft tries to drag its way through 20/50 as thick as treacle, but finally the bike grumbled to life and settles reluctantly to a steady idle as the oil begins to thin. My 1972 Moto Guzzi Eldorado is cold blooded even in the height of summer, so I left her on a fast idle while I assembled my riding gear for the attack on the winter roads. People make much of the side-to-side shake of the Guzzi V-twins, as if its something less than desirable, but really its part of their charm. Its as if she's breathing in anticipation.

Gearing up is quite an operation. My winter protection consists of two sets of long underwear and various shirts and fleece jackets, all squeezed into my fully quilted and lined riding suit. Forget about leather riding boots - you'd be flirting with frostbite. For this kind of riding you need to stuff your feet into a couple of pairs of wool socks inside fully lined Arctic winter boots. Not stylish perhaps, but effective. A balaclava under the helmet helps to stop the forehead from freezing and helps seal around the neck. Snowmobile mitts help keep the frost out of the fingers. Heated grips? You've got to be kidding!

The weather reports promised mild conditions for a few days, with sunshine most of the time and perhaps a few brief rain or snow showers - nothing much to get excited about. More importantly, the official Quebec road reports indicated that all the major highways between Ontario and the lower St. Lawrence River valley were clear and bare. I quickly filled up my panniers with extra clothes and enough tools do a complete roadside tear-down, strapped on my emergency sleeping bag, blankets and four-season hammock and hit the road.

Before I bought her my Guzzi had last seen the road in 1985. Between 1972 and 1985, she was ridden all over the North American continent, usually, and somewhat bizarrely towing a substantial camper trailer, complete with electric brakes controlled by a twist grip on the left handlebar. To achieve this trick, her owner had welded a 3/8 inch steel plate to the rear of the frame, and affixed a standard tow ball just behind the passenger seat. Other, less robust motorcycles might have been twisted out of shape by this kind of treatment, but not the loop-frame Guzzi, second cousin to the Ford 9n tractor! It's a peculiar arrangement, but since I also tow a (much smaller) trailer from time to time, I see no reason to change it. Its all part of the evolving patina of her character. I further modified it by welding on a couple of hollow rails which now support a detachable rear rack. It may not be pretty, indeed some might say its downright ugly, but it does the job. The previous owner had also fitted an external oil filter to keep the old girl cool while dragging the trailer around. It uses a spin-on filter compatible with just about all GC V6 engines, so I can get them at virtually any corner garage.

After 45,000 kilometers of hard use, the Guzzi's original chrome lined barrels started to flake so the previous owner had large bore cylinder replacements installed, increasing the bore from 83 mm to 88mm and displacement from a nominal 850ccs to just shy of a full litre. When I bought her, she had 56,000 kilometers on the clock.

Even though he stopped using the Guzzi in 1985, her first owner had cared enough to made sure that she was stored properly, so when I bought her in October 2007, although she was running roughly from gummy carburetors and had perished tires and shaggy springs, she was more or less good to go. Over the last year I have changed a few cables, replaced the brake shoes and tyres, upgraded the lighting switch, added new points, rotor and ht lines, renewed the car jets and needles and replaced the fork springs and rear drive seal.

Some people I've met think I should restore her to showroom condition and not expose her to salt-covered, rust inducing roads, or thrash the living daylights out of her on the highway, to which I say, "*She's not a Holy Relic*". Classic bikes were built to be used. They were not designed as toys, only to be ridden when the sun is shining, the chrome is gleaming and you have the matching, logo emblazoned leathers.

I figure the Eldorado has many thousands of kilometers of life left in her before she needs some real work. She'll certainly outlast me. As with many bikes of her vintage, her brakes are abysmal, but you learn to ride accordingly. Her handling is perfectly up to any riding I feel like doing, and I have yet to scrape any of her parts, and that includes her sidecar mounts (for when the weather really gets bad) which you would think would be the first to touch. As for comfort, even though she does her share of shaking and vibrating, I have had no trouble logging long days in the saddle.

Once I've clunked my way up through the gears, -and yes, everything they say about the agricultural nature of Guzzi gearboxes is true- she settles down to a steady rumble and by late morning a couple of hundred kilometers have passed beneath our wheels, I've crossed the Ottawa River which is still jammed with ice, and entered the Province of Quebec. My plan is to see how far east I can get until the weather deteriorates again, so I skirt behind Montreal and join the north shore of the St. Lawrence just west of Trois-Rivieres, spending the first night at a motel strategically located down-wind from the malodorous pulp mill.

In the morning, we burble along comfortably as we head down Highway 138, hugging the north shore of the river with the road pretty much to ourselves. Although the Montreal - Quebec City corridor is busy, most traffic sticks to the four-lane Highway 40, which also parallels the river, but just a little further to the north. This part of Quebec contains numerous small scenic villages, grand churches and architecturally interesting stone farmhouses, many of which have their origins in the seventeenth century. The stamp of the old French Seigneurial system is still plainly visible in the strip layout of the fields, which stretch from the edge of the river to the road, and which resemble flattened English ridge and furrow.

Even though the roads are completely clear, the amount of snow lying in the fields has been steadily increasing the further I travel east and north. I pass one cemetery where the tops of the gravestones are only just visible peeking out above the standing snow. In other places, the road-side snow banks are four or five feet high. The Guzzi's big screen keeps me out of the wind, and while the air is on the coolish side - hovering just one or two degrees above zero - I find I am good for two or three hours at a stretch between breaks.

Plenty of snow remaining in the cemetery in March

    Fortunately, there is an unwritten national law in Canada requiring a 'Tim Horton's' donut / coffee house at every crossroads - or at least, that's the way it seems - so there is usually somewhere to stop and warm up for a few minutes over a mug of coffee and a sugar and lard laden fritter.

    Beyond Quebec City, we enter the Charlevoix Region, the landscape becomes wilder, the Laurentian mountains crowd along the north shore of the river, and settlements are fewer and further between. The highway rises steeply across the heavily forested rocky shoulders of the mountains - at one point rising to 2440 feet above sea level - and falls into deeply glaciated valleys with metronome-like regularity. My bike has prodigious torque at any revs. On these roads, a slight opening of the throttle in top (5th) gear, has the bike roaring uphill with no evidence of complaint or strain. On the downhill stretches, the brakes are barely necessary as the engine scrubs off any excessive speed.

    Highway 138 comes to an abrupt stop 188 kilometers down river from Quebec City and about 300 kilometers into my day. A bend in the road suddenly exposes views of the Saguenay Fjord and before I'd really taken that in, I was gliding on to the ferry on-ramp.

The Guzzi attracted plenty of attention from the crew and passengers on the ferry, although because my French is limited to a single phrase, I couldn't tell whether they were laughing in admiration of the machine, or at the daftness of its rider. One fellow, who fortunately did speak English, looked long and hard at the bike before declaring that it was built like a car. He wasn't the least bit surprised to hear that various Fiat and VW. parts (starter, generator, distributor etc.) can be used as substitutes for pukka Guzzi parts, since they all picked from the same parts bin.

Towards Tadoussac (again)

The ferry to Tadoussac across the Saguenay Fjord

The small village of Tadoussac (population 855) lies on a headland on the north side of the Saguenay Fjord, where the waters of the Saguenay River mix with those of the St. Lawrence. This part of Quebec is one of extremes. Tadoussac, which was founded in 1600, is both the oldest continuously occupied settlement in Quebec and the oldest French settlement in the Americas. The St. Lawrence River, which has been tidal since Trois-Rivieres is astonishingly large - about 25 kilometers wide at this point - and the Saguenay Fjord, the most southerly in Quebec, and one of the longest in the world, extends inland through the Laurentian Mountains for more than 100 kilometers And as if to cap it all off, the area is well known for the prodigious numbers of whales which feed in the rich waters at the junction of the two water bodies. Beluga, minke, and the enormous fin and blue whales can often be seen in the area. Needless to say, I didn't see any!

I had been a bit disappointed to find out that the road between Tadoussac and the town of Saguenay didn't closely follow the north shore of the fjord, but instead followed a route to the north, well inland from the water. I shouldn't have been! Highway 172 should be on everyone's list of 'great motorcycling roads'. It bends, twists and loops between high wooded slopes, past sheer rocky outcrops, it skirts lake shores and follows rivers and creeks along its 78 mile path between the two communities. Other than the road itself, there are very few signs of human activity and only a handful of houses. I don't know what it would be like to ride on a modern sport bike, because with all the frost heaves, the road surface can be a bit .....er.....unsettling, but if you enjoy bumbling along at sane speeds, it is unequivocally magnificent.

I first noticed a few whisps of late afternoon cloud as I filled up with fuel at the only gas station on the road. The group of snowmobilers near the pumps gave me some astonished looks before blasting off up a snow covered side road on their machines. It may have been this that started me thinking about the weather. The previous night's forecast had shown a thin vertical band of storms moving east across the map towards Quebec. So far, I was still to their east, but I knew they would catch up with me sooner or later. I had been planning on staying in Saguenay but as I rode across the bridge into Chicoutimi, I decided to beat it south to Quebec City before the weather struck.

From the amount of snow lying in the forest and along the side of the roads, it was clear that any storm hitting the Saguenay region at this time of year was bound to come as snow, and snow would leave me completely stuck until the highway crews had time to get the roads clear and bare enough for two wheels again. That could take days.

Quebec City lies 177 kilometers due south of Saguenay, so enjoys a slightly milder climate. Perhaps, if I was really lucky and got a move on, I could get there before the storm hit, and if not, there was a good chance that any precipitation might only fall there as rain. By this point, my tally of kilometers for the day was edging close to 500, but since I could still feel my backside, another two hours in the saddle wouldn't be too hard to bear.

Highway 175 runs due south from Saguenay to Quebec City through the 4885 square mile *Reserve faunique des Laurentides* wilderness area. The highway is in the process of being converted to four lanes, so enormous rock cuts and construction camps line what is otherwise a beautiful route. Apart from a single gas station / restaurant at about the mid-way point the area is an uninhabited wilderness of rounded mountains, forests, lakes, rivers and valleys which have been protected since 1895 and a wildlife reserve since 1981. Fortunately there was little active construction and few other vehicles on the road, so I gave the Guzzi a little more throttle, cruising well above the speed limit.

As the daylight faded, the sky clouded over, and I noticed the first specks of rain on my visor about 45 kilometers north of Quebec City. At least, they were rain specks while I rode in the valleys, but every time the road rose up over the shoulder of one of the mountains, the rain turned to ice pellets which rattled on my helmet and windscreen. By good fortune, the precipitation stayed light, barely soaking the road and not accumulating as anything slippery or solid under the wheels. You can imagine my relief as I swung the Guzzi under the well lit portico at the Comfort Inn, switched her off, and went inside to register.

Even before I opened the curtains in the morning, I knew something had changed. There was a heavy softness to the light squeezing through the gaps, so I wasn't particularly surprised to find a good dusting of wet snow covering the bike and everything else within sight. The tv weather channel promised that the temperature was gradually going to rise through the morning, but with slush on all the roads for kilometers in all directions, there was no way I was going anywhere for a few hours.

By 10AM, the snow had stopped falling, and while they were sodden, the roads were no longer snow covered or slushy, so I strapped my gear on the bike, settled my account at the front desk and set out for home. Hoping to leave the urban area quickly, I joined a major through-way. I had hardly wound up through the gears when the bike spluttered, coughed, then cut out altogether. I coasted to a stop right where two sections of the highway joined, leaving me surrounded on both sides by heavy morning traffic, throwing up spray in all directions from the wet roads. Damn! The distributor and HT lines were dripping water, and when I cranked the bike over, I could see sparks tracking across the surface of the distributor cap.

As a sixteen year old, I had once abandoned my 1950 Panther 600 single at the side of a Scottish road when water got in to the electrics, only to be called up by the cops a couple of weeks later with the command to collect my perfectly good, fully functioning bike from their nice dry storage shed. From that youthful experience, I had learned that one only had to wait long enough for the engine heat to dry the electrics and I could be on my way again. As long as I didn't get creamed by the traffic streaming by me on both sides first - that is.

The bike had no sooner struggled back to life when a *Surety du Quebec* Ford Crown Victoria pulled up behind me, blue lights flashing. It didn't take much High School English for the policemen to make it politely, but abundantly clear to me that they though I was a complete idiot to be out on a motorbike on such a day. Nevertheless, after checking my papers to make sure I wasn't a Hell's Angel who had somehow escaped the province-wide crime sweep reported on the news that morning, they handed me my papers, suggested I get on to less heavily traveled roads, and wished me well.

Throughout my time talking to the police, the Guzzi had been idling steadily as if nothing had ever been the matter, so by the time I started off again, the electrics were good and dry. Apart from a couple of splutters a few kilometers down the road, she ran flawlessly for the remainder of the trip.

Forty kilometers west of Quebec City, I reached the trailing edge of the weather formation that had brought the snow, the skies cleared, and the temperature gradually rose until it was well into the single digits above zero and feeling positively mild. Since the bike was running well and the roads were becoming dry, I joined Highway 40, steamed through the middle of Montreal on the expressway and stayed on the four lane highway virtually the whole way home. The Old Bike Lover in me thinks I should be nursing the old bike along gentle back roads instead of thrashing her down a major continental arterial road. But the Practical Motorcyclist in me realises that the old Guzzi is just as much in her element droning along the highway at 75 mph for hour after hour, as she is bumbling along back roads at barely above an idle.

Within a few days of returning to Ontario, another storm system drifted through, the province was once again blanketed in snow, and the bike was again languishing in the garage. I dallied briefly with the idea of bolting on the sidecar for a while, but in the end decided that since I'd been lucky with my three stolen days, I had better be patient for a while, at least until the road crews had done their work and the tarmac was bare and dry once more.

Spring eventually arrives. The snow banks disappear, the robins and geese return, and eventually the pretty sport bikes and cruisers are back out on the roads, and there is no longer any need to hunt for those stolen days - until next winter.

Covered bridge between Tadoussac and Saguenay

THE TRANS-LABRADOR HIGHWAY

In 2009, the Trans-Labrador Highway was finally completed, linking Labrador City to the east coast at the coastal village of Mary's Harbour. From Mary's Harbour the coast road leads south to the ferry across to the island of Newfoundland. Suddenly it was possible to do a circle ride from Ontario, through Quebec and across the Labrador plateau, returning via Newfoundland, another ferry over to Nova Scotia and the long haul back to Ontario on the Trans-Canada Highway. Although now rapidly becoming paved, in 2012 most of the route was still unpaved, with hundreds of kilometers on rough gravel and dirt through uninhabited wilderness, including one section of about 410 kilometers between places where fuel was available.

Most people seem to feel that a modern 'adventure' bike is necessary for this trip, but my first ride up to Labrador City convinced me that both the bike and I were perfectly suited to completing the 6000 kilometer ride. The Eldorado had proven her reliability. With carbs, points and simple electrics, I convinced myself that short of a catastrophic mechanical failure, there was little I couldn't fix at the side of the road..............

DAY 1: *Inverary Ontario to La Malbaie, Quebec 718kms.*

The unwholesome reality of Montreal lies directly in a line between where I live and where I want to go. There are two main options - suffer through the urban nightmare, or find a way around. I usually choose the latter.

From Inverary I rode through rural eastern Ontario to Hawkesbury on the Ottawa River. Crossing in to Quebec, I followed a more-or-less direct loop around the back of Montreal, passing through Lachute, Joliette and Berthierville, joining Highway 138 along the north shore of the St. Lawrence River about 30kms southwest of Trois Rivieres and well east of Montreal.

It was Saturday, so just about every cruiser and Can-Am Spider (the national toy of Quebec) was out along 138. On any normal day, 138 is a really nice road. It hugs the river and passes by classic 18th century Quebec farmhouses and exuberant churches, through a seigneurial landscape divided into long, narrow strips extending back from the river frontage.

I have ridden that route many times but that Saturday it was too hot and there was too much traffic for my taste. The Guzzi was running well and I was eager to get this first day over with so I joined the arterial Highway 40 and blasted through Quebec City, rejoining the river just east of Beauport. On trips like this, I always start off wondering whether its reasonable to thrash a 39 year old bike along major highways at highway speeds for hour after hour. After I while though, the lazy cadence of the engine and the effortless and comfortable way she eats up the kilometers convinces me that I have no need to be concerned.

Beyond the religious pilgrimage centre at St. Anne de Beaupre, 138 runs across the shoulders of the Laurentian Mountains, through scenery which, while not grand, is delightful. It rises over high ground, well inland from the river, through a series of small strip villages before dropping down to the pretty little town of Baie St. Paul where the Geoffrey River meets the St. Lawrence. It comes as a bit of a surprise to many to find that this part of Quebec is so unilingually French. My French is limited to "*Je ne parle pas francais*" but I get along just fine with grunts, pointing and judicious use of my visa card. People are pretty much the same the world over, and if two people have a desire to communicate, whether they share a language in common or not, they can. That, at least, has been my experience.

My circuitous route around Montreal had eaten up quite some time, and it was well into the early evening before I reached La Malbaie. I had ridden about 750 kilometers, but with the heat and traffic, it felt like much more. I resorted to a motel I had stayed in once before. If I'm feeling charitable, I could describe it as a worker's motel - it was one of those places that has a parking lot full of trucks with work trailers and tandem trucks. If I'm being honest, I would call it sleazy.

DAY 2: **La Malbaie to 100km south of Labrador City: 784kms**.

I was making an early start so I wheeled the Guzzi close to the road before starting the engine. While blasting (a relative term) down the highway through Quebec City yesterday, I had blown out most of the chicken wire I use as exhaust baffles, so the bike was a tad loud.

Its only about 75 kilometers between La Malbaie and the ferry across the Saguenay Fjord to Tadoussac, but it's a nice ride. High forested hills and steep rocky bluffs crowd the road. It was overcast and dreary and I had stopped to put my rain gear on, but by the time I arrived at the ferry, it had cleared up a bit.

Baie Comeau lies almost 200 kilometers further to the north-east along the St. Lawrence River. Even though it's an enjoyable ride, I
wanted this part of the journey to be over. As far as I was concerned, the trip didn't really start until I hit gravel north of Manic 5.

From Baie Comaeu the route veers north away from the St.

Lawrence River in to the heart of Quebec, paralleling the Manicouagan River. Hydro Quebec has built a massive series of power dams on the river (Manic 1, 2, 3 and 5 - 4 was abandoned). The river flows south from the Manicouagan Reservoir which occupies the basin left by the impact of a 5km. diameter meteor. The crater is approximately 100 kms wide and can clearly be seen from space.

Highway 389 is a great road. It twists and turns through classic Canadian Shield country, crossing innumerable streams, avoiding rocky hills and lakes on its path between Baie Comeau and Manic 5. The road surface is in poor condition, with numerous frost heaves and potholes, but the scenery and endless curves more than compensate.

There is a gas station, cafe and motel at Manic 5. I needed to fill both the bike and my belly so I stopped first at the cafe. Three BMWs were lined up out front; a GS with the full Ewan/Charlie kit, an older RT and a modern paralever naked I didn't recognise. Their owners, who I think were probably out for a Sunday ride from Baie Comeau, were coming out of the cafe as I arrived, and I think it would be a bit of an understatement to say they were surprised to see the Guzzi and even more surprised when they learned where I was heading.

They were curious to find out whether I had any real idea of what was ahead. I like to think their concerns were assuaged once they learned that I had already ridden the 350 kms of gravel road between Manic 5 and Labrador City in both directions - and on the same Guzzi on an earlier trip, but if they were, it wasn't showing on their faces.

I rode the gravel road north from Manic 5 for about 200 kilometers that afternoon. The road was in fairly good condition - indeed, the short section of old paved road around the former location of the mining town of Gagnon was actually less pleasant to ride because it has become heavily frost heaved and has not been maintained well. As evening approached, I began to look for a place to camp. I travel with a 4 season Clark Jungle Hammock, so all I needed was a couple of trees approximately 8 feet part: generally not too much of a problem in this part of Quebec.

I found a small track leading to a lake, just off the side of the highway. I pitched my hammock, enjoyed a supper consisting of potato chips, baguette and beer, and settled in for the night to the mellifluous sound of courting loons.

Camping spot south of Labrador City

DAY 3: *100km south of Labrador City to Happy Valley / Goose Bay. 634 kms.*

I awoke to light shining through the bug screen straight into my eyes. "Must be dawn", I thought, unzipped the screen and struggled out for a pee. Then I noticed that vicious orb in the sky, looking balefully down on me. It wasn't dawn at all - just high moon. The moon has never been my friend and has always been a trigger for restlessness and insomnia. Thinking that dawn couldn't be far away, I had a quick snack, packed up the hammock and sleeping bags (I carry two lightweights which give me a wide range of temperature control) and got back on the bike.

It's at times like this that you notice the differences between modern bikes and those from the primordial past. The Eldorado's headlight (actually a 7 inch right-side car sealed beam) cast a weak pool of light a few feet in front of the front wheel. I switched to high beam and there was an ominous flickering before the pool expanded slightly. Still, with the combination of the moonlight and the headlight, there was enough illumination for me to navigate back on to the road and head for Labrador City. Surely dawn could not be far away?

This part of Highway 389 criss-crosses the railway tracks which lead south from the Fermont mine, just on the Quebec side of the Quebec / Labrador border. I had to be careful near the tracks, not because of any danger from trains, but because of the steeply rutted curves before and after every crossing. If I tried to go too fast, I could easily loose track of where the road was heading, and veer towards the ditch. On one of these corners, my high-beam quit altogether, temporarily leaving me to navigate by moonlight alone. I switched to low beam, adjusted my already desultory speed, and carried on.

Eventually the lights of the Fermont mine appeared in the distance, and beyond that, the paved road to Labrador City. I arrived in town just in time to be caught up in the 5:30AM, Tim Horton's pre-shift rush moment. By the time I had struggled out of my riding gear, the line-up was gone and I was able to order a coffee and breakfast sandwich unimpeded.

Beyond Labrador City, the road is paved for quite a distance. Nice road. No traffic. Perfect surface. The landscape is fairly flat supporting stunted spruce trees and string bog interspersed with innumerable ponds and small lakes. I'm assuming that the plan is to pave the whole thing eventually. For me, that will be a shame, for no matter how quiet a paved road may be, it just doesn't provide the same sense of remoteness that a gravel one does - and I'm assuming that I'm not alone in having those feelings.

The old Eldorado continued to roll along uncomplainingly. I had filled with gas in Labrador City, so was fairly confident that I could reach Churchill Falls, a mere 244 kilometers away without having to resort to my spare tank. Once the road reverted to gravel, my speed decreased and my fuel consumption increased, especially because this section of the road was undergoing some fairly heavy maintenance, including laying kilometers of fresh, loose gravel - the motorcyclists bane. I guess the work crews and signal flag people aren't used to seeing an elderly Moto Guzzi on the Trans-Lab. I either got incredulous looks or enthusiastic thumbs-up and waves.

In Churchill Falls I refilled my tank and bought some wholesome and sustaining food to keep me going on the next leg of the journey.

Before I left Ontario, I had remounted the Eldo's generator and applied Locktite to the bolt threads. The generator sits in a cradle between the cylinders. The bolts that hold the cradle to the engine block are a weak spot on these bikes - and sometimes even the cradle will crack with vibration. Somewhere between Churchill Falls and Happy Valley, it became obvious that the generator was flopping around again and all my preparation had been for nought. This might sound as though it could have been a bit of a problem, but a well positioned bungee cord soon had the generator more or less held in place.

Common practice is to run 30wt fork oil or ATF (automatic transmission fluid) in the forks of these Loop Frame Guzzis. Before I had left, however, I had read somewhere that running 80/90 gear oil in the forks improved damping and their general feel. I'm glad I did. Some parts of the highway were potholed or had long sections of washboard.

My forks would occasionally bottom out, but not nearly as often as I had expected.

The 290+ kilometers to Happy Valley/Goose Bay passed uneventfully. For me, these road trips are all about flow. I imagine I'm tuned in to the sound of the engine, the feel of the road surface beneath the tyres, how my backside is coping and whether I'm getting close to running out of fuel, but usually I can't remember a single thought during hours of riding. And that's just the way I like it.

About 60 kilometers west of Happy Valley the road suddenly dove off the edge of the Labrador plateau into the valley of the Churchill River. From here to town, the road has been paved with the most perfect asphalt I think I have ever seen. Those last few kilometers into Happy Valley were sheer bliss.

DAY 4: *Happy Valley / Goose Bay to Port Hope-Simpson. 409 kms.*

Before leaving Happy Valley I had to find some replacement gloves for the pair I had accidentally left at the side of the road once the pavement started, and fill up with gas again. The young lad who served me in the Home Hardware, really surprised me by saying "*nice Guzzi*", until I noticed the massive patch of road rash on his arm and the old Yamaha parked outside. Clearly he had recently had a lesson in the need for proper protective clothing.

It is 409 kms (254 miles) from Happy Valley to Port Hope-Simpson - the most recently completed section of the Trans-Labrador Highway and the longest stretch between gas supplies. I was fairly confident that with the extra 10 litres I was carrying in the can on my back-rack, I would have enough - but it would be close.

I was expecting the newest section of highway to be a nasty mess of fresh, loose 3inch aggregate and had been steeling myself for some slow and painful riding. The reality was quite different. The new road (Highway 510) diverges from Highway 520 a few kilometers out of town and almost immediately crosses the Churchill River via a long bridge. The road bed on the bridge has been constructed of welded re-bar by someone with a death wish towards motorcyclists. The ribs of the bridge surface grabbed at my front tyre and shook it like a terrier with a rat the whole way across. Perhaps most of the riders who travel this route on 'adventure' bikes, sail over this bridge without noticing its evil inclinations. I'd be interested to hear.

Beyond the bridge, the road was in excellent condition. I had already noticed that those sections of the Trans-Lab which were constructed from crushed rock aggregate tended to be less pleasant and motorcycle friendly than those made from aggregate derived by sorting and sifting local glacial till. The natural materials pack down into a smooth (usually reddish) surface, providing a wonderful road surface which could be ridden at virtually any speed, even on a jalopy like mine. In contrast, even when well packed, the road surface left by the man-made materials was a constant mine-field of loose gravel patches which sit like marbles on a billiard table.

Today the weather was a bit grim with dull leaden skies and the promise of rain. A little rain wouldn't be a bad thing since it would dampen down the dust and help consolidate the loose gravel. Too much rain though, would turn the gravel dust to mud and create a whole new set of riding issues. Fortunately for me, it didn't do that, although it did rain hard enough for me to stop, put on my industrial strength rain gear and hide my video camera.

Since I am fairly tall, the standard screen on the Guzzi isn't quite high enough to shield me from turbulence - especially at highway speeds. Much to the distain of my motorcycle riding son, my solution is to duct tape an old helmet visor to the top of the screen. Despite looking like a dog's breakfast, it works remarkably well.

Initially, I had taken it off once I hit gravel, but with the higher speeds possible on the excellent road south of Happy Valley, and for added protection from the rain, I decided to remount it - a laborious process that takes perhaps two whole minutes. I immediately noticed an improvement in my riding in the softer gravel sections. The higher screen forced me to look further ahead; whereas before I was probably looking 10-15 feet in front of my wheel, now I had to scan the road at least 20 feet ahead, and usually further.

It was about this time that I started to notice some unusual tracks - narrow half moon shapes which diverged from the heavily flattened areas where the majority of the vehicle tracks ran. After another hundred kilometers, they became more common and now I could begin to trace more of a linear path. Something was heading down the road, leaving tracks no more than an inch or two wide. On the straight stretches they were hard to follow. Up hill they were easier to trace as they seemed to weave from side to side.

I gradually became certain I was following a bicycle. What kind of a person would ride a road like this? I soon found out as I eventually caught up with him about 120 kms past where his tracks clearly showed he had spent the night. The cyclist was a 58 year old gentleman from Gatineau, Quebec. He had been on the road many days. I pulled up next to him and after brief hellos, handed him two bottles of beer from my pack. Once, cycling in Spain in the seventies, I had been the recipient of a similar unexpected kindness.

Just when you start thinking you're a bit of a hero for riding so far you meet someone like this: One Tough Dude!

The last few kilometers before reaching the Labrador coast brought a considerable change in the scenery. The endless spruce forest, interspersed with large areas of bog gave way to a bare, rolling landscape of krummholz and lichen. The influence of the cold Labrador current in the nearby waters was plainly evident.

As on previous days, the Eldorado had behaved flawlessly. As I parked in front of the hotel in Port Hope-Simpson, I wondered whether the riders of the expedition equipped KLR's parked outside had enjoyed as pleasant, comfortable and trouble free journey as me.

Hotel - Mary's Harbour

DAY 5: *Port Hope-Simpson to Port au Choix. 339 kms.*

I left Port Hope-Simpson early. I had enjoyed supper with the two KLR riders in the hotel the previous evening - one an experienced dirt rider, the other not. I think the bikes were bought especially for the trip. Regardless, they seemed to be enjoying their big adventure and didn't seem put out by a garrulous old geezer and his antique Italian steed.

This section of road traverses rolling terrain inland from the Labrador coast for 140 kilometres and the village of Red Bay. Trees cling in a few small hollows. The rest of the land is bare rock, krummholz and moss. This may be the country Jacques Cartier described in 1534 as *'The Land God Gave to Cain'* but I loved it. Unfortunately, I can't say the same for the road.

Potholes and puddles, heading to the coast

Generally I'm fond of gravel and dirt roads - indeed, in the part of eastern Ontario where I live, I regularly search them out for some 'Eldo Abuse', but this stretch of road was a nasty mess of potholes and washboard with just enough good sections to get you sped up and to lulled into increasing speed and looking at the scenery before the next grim patch hit.

The constant jarring had worked the generator bolts completely loose, and while it was still functioning properly, held roughly in position by its centering pin and my bungee, it was clearly time for a fix. Nevertheless, I ploughed on, eating a perfectly respectable breakfast at a hotel in Mary's Harbour, and visiting the Parks Canada Basque whaling exhibit in Red Bay. When I'm on a riding trip, I generally make it a policy not to stop at cultural attractions, since such things are far too redolent of how I make a living. But my wife had worked on some of the textiles from the excavations and I wanted to see whether they were on display (they were). Glad I did actually - the interpreters were charming.

When I left home a few days earlier I had been aware of a slight toothache. Almost inevitably, it had become increasingly annoying as the journey proceeded, so that by the time I got to Mary's Harbour, I was in constant pain. That first sip of hot coffee with breakfast triggered what felt like an electric shock right up my tooth and into my eyeball. I somehow managed to drink the rest of the coffee and eat the bacon and eggs, mostly by chewing on the other side of my mouth, but it wasn't fun. Eventually I located a pharmacy and was able to buy some *Ambesol*, which gave me some relief for the rest of the trip. However, my obvious need for some dental attention, rather blunted my enjoyment of the last couple of days and hastened my journey home.

Below Red Bay, the road is paved as far as the ferry at Blanc Sablon. It stays near the coast, passing through a number of small villages, which create the illusion that the whole area is well populated. It's a delusion. Settlement is strictly limited to the narrow band along the coast. The interior is solely the domain of caribou and blackflies.

I arrived at the ferry dock with a couple of hours to spare, so I thought I would finally get to grips with the generator problem. One of the great things about really getting to know a bike is that you can strip it down virtually anywhere without a second thought. I know which wrenches fit which bolts and had made sure I brought them in my tool kit.

Within a few minutes the bike was naked and next to it was an increasingly large pile of gear and motorcycle parts. Both the tank and seat had to come off, then the aluminum generator so I could free the belt. Once the bungee was unhooked I could see just how loose the retaining bolts had become (very), so I removed the generator - or more strictly speaking, moved it aside so I didn't have to undo the wiring - and set about tightening the bolts which hold its cradle to the engine cases between the cylinders. It's a tight fit to get at those bolts, but I thought I had done a creditable job of tightening them. Turns out I was wrong.

Once I was done, I rode the bike up to near the ferry office to wait until they would deign to sell us tickets. Don had just arrived on his 1994 GS, leaking from both fork seals and drooling from a front caliper. After swapping road stories for a while, I started to have some sympathy for the bike. He had ridden the Trans-Lab a heck of a lot faster than I, and had arrived at Blanc Sablon, from BC, via Yellowknife.

The ferry crossing was pleasant, calm and uneventful and we arrived on the Newfoundland side just as the sun was going down. I briefly considered staying at the local hotel, but the line-up to sign in convinced me that I would be better off finding somewhere to hang my hammock. I rode on in the increasing darkness, keeping and eye out for moose and periodically checking out likely spots, but I guess I was getting finicky since nothing met my requirements. In the end, I took the side road in to Port au Choix and settled in to a dismal, and somewhat overpriced motel.

DAY 6: *Port au Choix to ferry at Port aux Basques. 500 kms.*

I wasn't ready for Newfoundland. I hadn't been able to see much the night before when I rode from the ferry to Port au Choix, but now it was light and the sun was shining. Originally I had intended to spend a few days exploring western Newfoundland, but within a couple of hours, I threw that idea out of the metaphorical window.

The road south was wonderful; nice pavement, wonderful scenery. The Gulf of the St. Lawrence lies to the west, the Long Range Mountains - the long chain of low hills which form the spine of the Northern Peninsula - to the east. The road hugs the coast, passing by a number of small fishing villages such as Bellburns, Daniel's Harbour and Parson's Pond which, because they are oriented to the sea, are barely touched by the highway. I was impressed by the virtual absence of roadside development. Long may it remain that way. Too many scenic roads have been ruined by unregulated strip development.

Mist shrouded my first view of the Gros Morne Mountains. I could see the shape of the table-top massif looming over the coast. As I rode closer, the mist lifted and I enjoyed excellent views of this World Heritage Site. From Rocky Harbour the road turns inland, seemingly through the heart of the mountains, rising high over forested mountain shoulders before diving down to lakeshore. It is a wonderful road through remarkable scenery, made even more pleasant by the relative lack of traffic and the absence of gimcrackery.

At the top of one long climb, I pulled into a rest stop / picnic overlook and cruised to a stop. Only one other person was there - his tent discretely set up to one side, and he was sitting at one of the picnic tables.

"Is that a 750 or an 850" he said, as soon as I had switched off the engine.

"It's a 1000 now" I replied, *"but it used to be an 850".*

"Ah, so its an Eldorado, not an Ambassador!"

What are the chances that the only person at a rest stop atop the Gros Morne Mountains would speak Moto Guzzi? Bill and I swapped Guzzi knowledge and lies for a few minutes, I snapped a couple of pictures then I hit the road again.

Selfie in Gros Morne National Park, Newfoundland

At Deer Lake I joined the Trans-Canada Highway - the single tarmac thread that extends from St. John's on the east coast of Newfoundland, to Victoria, on Vancouver Island, British Columbia, off the west coast of the continent. Not surprisingly, this is a large highway with some divided sections. I was conscious of an extra vibration at certain rpms, and assumed that the generator had managed to do its magic on the mounting bolts again. Never mind - she was still humming along nicely, and had no trouble matching the ambient traffic speed - where there was any traffic at all.

I reached Channel Port aux Basques in the late afternoon. It's a pretty little town, completely dominated by the ferry terminal, but with a host of small wooden houses scattered seemingly at random across the small headland overlooking picturesquely named Shark Cove.

I rode around the winding streets for a while then headed to Canadian Tire for some essentials: another bungee, some heavy duty cable ties, some 1/8th inch aircraft wire and clamps. That bloody generator was going to get clamped within an inch of its life! After about 20 minutes in the parking lot, I had the thing fixed to my satisfaction. It looked a bit like a rats nest, but the generator could no longer bounce around.

The ferry started to load at about 7PM but didn't leave the dock until 9. That left plenty of time for something to eat and a couple of beers to help me sleep. I managed to get a couple of hours of sporadic sleep in one of the recliners on the rear deck as the ferry glided over amazingly quiet waters towards North Sydney, Nova Scotia.

FINAL DAY: *North Sydney, Nova Scotia to Invermay, Ontario. 1755 kms.*

By 2:30AM, I was out of the ferry and in a line of traffic heading out of town along the Trans-Canada Highway. Just about everyone stopped at the first Tim Horton's coffee shop, and many, including me, were disappointed to find that only the drive-through was in operation. I didn't really have a clear plan at this point, but since it was chilly, I took the opportunity to put on my riding suit, checked the status of my fuel, and headed off down the highway.

At first it was busy with ferry traffic, so the dim glimmer from my low beam wasn't really an issue. Gradually though, the traffic thinned and I had to rely on my own marginal light source for navigation. Blessedly, there were no nocturnal insects, so I was able to shed my eye protection and venture naked into the night.

I love riding at night, even if I could barely see where I was going. There is little to distract me from the road ahead (what I could see of it) and I had the accompaniment of the wonderful, clatter from the tappets of that glorious v-twin, and the booming sound from her pipes.

Before dawn, the Eldo started to stutter - the inevitable sign of fuel starvation. Usually, while she's still complaining, I just reach down to the right side of the tank, turn on the secondary petcock and carry on using the reserve supply. This time though, with no idea how many kilometres I would have to cover until I found an open gas station, I opted to stop and pour in the contents of my 10 litre auxiliary supply.

I saw nothing of Nova Scotia except that black ribbon of road. Another time! By the time I got to New Brunswick it was light, I had eaten some breakfast and found some fuel, so I was able to enjoy the wide relaxing highway and the higher permitted cruising speeds.

At the Quebec border, the road reverted to two lanes and roadworks, more or less all the way to Riviere du Loup on the St. Lawrence River. By this point I had ridden just over 1000 kilometres since the ferry and may have been getting a bit punch-drunk.

"Heck, I'm almost home" I shouted to myself (I'm not sure whether this was out loud or not - it had been a long day.........).

The last 700 kilometres are a bit of a blur. Highway 20, past Quebec City and Drummondville to Montreal is a big, wide highway, busy with Friday afternoon traffic. I stuck to the inside lane, traveling slightly below Quebec's normal highway speed of 120+ kph. I hovered around

103 kph (GPS speed - 78 mph on my Veglia speedo!) which the Eldorado seems to like just fine for hours.

Interestingly, I saw many of the vehicles which sped past me many times over. They would go racing past in Mercs, BMWs and the occasional Harley, while I plodded along like a tortoise. A couple of hours later, there they would be again, looking somewhat perplexed as to how I had got ahead of them. Some distinctive cars passed me at least three times.

I didn't want to have to worry about fuel while traversing Montreal, so I filled up in Drummondville. I don't mind riding in traffic, but Montreal has such a convoluted system of through-ways that I wanted no distractions. As it turned out, I was able to sail through Montreal without any difficulty, although it took its toll on my stamina.

By the time the urban area was behind me and I had made it to the Ontario border it was pitch black again and heading towards midnight. I could tell I was starting to loose concentration, even arguing with myself as to whether I was awake and conscious of reality, or already asleep. Not a good sign! I pulled off at the first service station and slugged back a large coffee. That, and the cool night air did the trick for a while, although by Prescott I was beginning to flag again. A second cup of coffee and a few minutes off the bike seemed to work. I rode the last 100 kilometres in a state of hyper-real focus and concentration, pulling in to my driveway at 1:30AM - 22 hours (adjusting for the time zone I'd crossed) after I'd left the ferry terminal in Nova Scotia.

Tired? You bet!

A NEW BIKE

Life is full of highs and lows. One moment I was sitting on the couch feeling sorry for myself, nursing a couple of broken ribs, cursing the cold March weather and my general misfortune: the next, I was excitedly heading down the snow covered highway to Quebec to look at a bike.

A few days earlier I had been lazing in the bathtub re-reading some of my favourite motorcycle magazines. I put my hand on the side of the tub, stood up, then fell sideways as I slipped on the wet porcelain, smashing my ribs against the tub edge with the full weight of my body. My wife Chris was in her office in the spare bedroom. She heard the crash and my groan as all the air was driven from my lungs. By the time she arrived, I was breathing again, but it was obvious to both of us that I had done something nasty to myself. Those of you who have had broken ribs know that the only effective cure is time and rest. Any movement or laughter is immensely painful.

The following week, while recuperating on the couch, feeling bored, I decided to post an advert in the local classifieds: *'Wanted, older Moto Guzzi for restoration'*. I had barely posted it when my laptop pinged, announcing an incoming email. A gentleman in Quebec had a 1974 Moto Guzzi 750 for sale, non-runner, was I interested? You bet! I figured driving my van wasn't all that different to sitting on the couch, so within a few minutes I had hitched up the trailer (that didn't feel good at all) and was heading east. Before I'd left I had quickly researched the bike. It was described as a 750S - a transitional, one year model only made in 1974 shortly after Alejandro De Tomaso took control of the company. It was never imported into North America. Reputedly only 948 were ever made - a rare bird indeed.

As soon as I saw the bike, I knew it was going home on the trailer. Never mind the rusted out seat pan, the torn leather seat, its general tattiness and the knowledge that I would almost certainly have to spend the best part of $1000 over and above the purchase price to replace the original cylinders which, after sitting so long, would have flaky and bearing-destroying chrome lining. To my eyes it was gorgeous. After some brief, good natured haggling, we agreed upon a price, got it on to the trailer (ouch again), and I headed home.

Any motorcycle that has been around for 40 years is likely to have a bit of a history and this one was no exception. The previous owner - an old British car restorer - had acquired it in partial trade against some work he had completed for a client, and although he had registered it in

Quebec, he had no desire or interest in getting it running. He just wanted it out of the way. Before him, it had reputedly sat in a heated basement for the last twenty-five years.

Still on the trailer

The first thing I noticed was that the frame and engine numbers didn't match. That alone isn't too surprising. Moto Guzzi never matched engine and frame numbers. However, while the engine number (VK*033954*), the overall styling of the bike, and many of the details and fittings indicated 750S, the frame (VK*12340*) was from a 1972 Moto Guzzi V7 Sport. Technically that isn't an issue: frames of the V7 Sport and the 750S are identical and it is only an issue if you're an anorak. Still, mine may be the only 1972 registered 750S in existence! Clearly though, there was something odd here. I turned to the wisdom of the Moto Guzzi cognoscenti on the WildGuzzi forum for some help.

In the meantime, I pulled the carbs and dropped them off with Ross Poulter at K-Tech Moto Services in Kingston for ultrasound cleaning. Then I attacked the engine. The cross-the-frame Guzzi V-twin is simplicity itself to work on. With the cylinders sticking out in the air, you just pull them apart. There are no head steadies to unbolt. You don't need to move the fuel tank. Just disconnect the carbs and the exhausts, unbolt the allen bolts holding the valve covers, remove the valve gear, then unbolt the heads.

The heads were in remarkably good condition. I checked for leakage around the valves - there was none, and the valve guides were still shiny and snug, suggesting that the engine had never been run much. The speedometer only showed just 7700 kilometres on the clock. Could this be true?

The cylinder bores were shiny and looked in good condition, but I wasn't interested in taking any chances. Some of the early V-twin Guzzis had chrome lining on the cylinders which can flake off, destroying the engine. The gurus at Wildguzzi instructed me to use a magnet to check the composition of the bores. Strongly magnetic: iron liners, very mildly magnetic: Nikasil lined, not magnetic at all: chrome lined. I thought I detected some very mild magnetism, but wasn't sure, but when I reported to the guys on Wildguzzi that the magic words '*Gilardoni*' were stamped in to the base of the cylinders, I was assured that they were definitely Nikasil. I rejoiced!

After draining the old oil and cleaning the oil pan, I refilled the sump with 20/50, reassembled the engine, retrieved the now shiny carbs from Ross, made sure the gas was flowing, attached a battery to the bike with some jumper cables and turned the key. To my complete astonishment, the 750S immediately burst into life, then settled down to a steady idle. Clearly, having the carbs cleaned ultrasonically had been a really good idea.

Over the following weeks, experts from a variety of locations around the world had me looking all over the bike for arcane details. In particular, Axel Bellmatx in southern France - a widely acknowledged expert in the history and details of early 750 Guzzis (V7 Sport, 750S, 750S3) - provided a host of things for me to investigate and check. What started to emerge was that the bike was a mixture of bits and pieces from both the V7 Sport and the 750S, some of which made sense and some of which didn't.

I had been hoping that the bike was a factory bitza - a bike thrown together in Mandello as a 750S, but using 'off the shelf'' parts to complete a production run. Axel showed me that this was unlikely. The frame indicated that it was from early in the V7 Sport series (series 1). Curiously, the whole front end of the bike: the forks with the eagle imprint on the fork leg (the V7 Sport forks have 'Moto Guzzi' stamp), the twin disk Brembo brakes, front mudguard and stays, bars and instruments were all identified as pure 750S. I struggled to visualize any accident that could result in so much damage to the frame that it needed to be replaced, yet left the forks intact and the engine cases unmarked. Sharp eyes on the Wildguzzi forum also noticed that the fuel tank had been repainted at some point, slightly diverging from (and in my opinion, improving) the original 750S's pattern of stripes. The side panels were pure 750S.

The silencers should be black chrome 'shark gill' pattern, not the barely-baffled Lafranconi 'Riservato Competizione' shiny chrome versions on mine, but they could have rotted out and in need of replacement at any time. Axel provided a couple of possible scenarios. Since the bike was now in North America, and had been for quite a while, he suggested that it could have been rebuilt using the V7 Sport frame to solve some importation / documentation issue. Alternatively, it might have been rebuilt with a frame bought as a spare to get around the loss of the bikes ownership title. Whatever the truth of its origins, I am in possession of a fine, elegant motorcycle; one that is regarded by many as one of the best looking 'cafe' style bikes ever produced. While it would be nice to have a completely original bike, in some ways it's a blessing. When I ride it, I don't feel as though I am abusing some holy relic.

In order to get the 750S back on the road, I replaced the seized front brake calipers with replacements from MgCycle(MgCycle.com), put on new Bridgestone Spitfire tyres, new tubes and reproduction "Stucci" seat, replaced the handlebar switch gear with a modern 'all in one' unit and added some air filters to the previously unfiltered carbs. The original switches were badly corroded, but I have kept them in a box, along with all the other parts I've replaced, so that forty or fifty years from now, if someone wants to return it to original, they can.

A thing of beauty..........

And what a bike it is! In 1974 it was one of the fastest bikes in production, and is still plenty fast, although compared to many modern motorcycles, its performance is no longer outstanding. Nevertheless, it accelerates with authority and is entirely happy to break most national speed limits with a couple of gears to spare. The tall gearing means that maintaining a high speed for long periods of time is effortless. I have no intentions of exploring its full performance potential: it is plenty fast enough for me. In fact, it's the only bike with which I have managed to collect a speeding ticket. The low handlebars and smooth, relaxed engine encourage a little bit of hooliganism.

The riding position must have been designed by a gibbon. The adjustable swan-neck clip-on handlebars encourage a forward lean and best suit those who are long in the arm, while the foot pegs are mid-mounted and set quite high, so anyone this side of stumpy, will find their knees are tightly bent. Even so, as a normally proportioned geriatric of 62 and 6'2", once my back has capitulated and loosened up to the long stretch, riding time is more determined by the thinness of the saddle than the peculiar stretch to the bars. I have ridden 600 mile days and still been able to walk.

With safety inspection, registration and insurance papers in my wallet, I started the inevitable process of determining the bike's reliability. From home, I began riding larger and larger circles, returning each time to do minor tweaks and adjustments. My regular 60 mile Sunday breakfast runs quickly expanded into day-long loops around eastern Ontario as my confidence in the bike grew. By the end of the summer I had no hesitation about loading my camping gear and setting off for a 400 mile ride up to the annual Ontario Moto Guzzi Riders Rally in Lavigne, northern Ontario. Fortunately, my confidence was rewarded. The bike performed flawlessly, happily droning along for hours at a steady 65 mph following the south bank of the Ottawa River along Highway 17.

The following year I ventured further afield. From my home near Kingston, Ontario it's about 1600 kilometres to the end of Highway 138 in Quebec. Since I like exploring Canada's 'ends of roads', it seemed the perfect way to do a little exploration and a nice, long, easy ride to see how the 750S managed a longer trip.

HIGHWAY 138 TO NATASHQUAN

Why would anyone choose a 38 year old sport bike for a manic blast up one of the more remote roads in Canada? It's a question I asked myself many times as I was riding home, fighting constant headwinds, the muscles in my neck and back screaming for relief, my backside feeling as though I was back in the headmasters office in Grammar School, and my knees locked in a permanent crook.

Of course, I'm exaggerating a bit. I actually find riding the 750S relatively comfortable - at least for sane distances - and while, after a few hours it does remind me that a) I am no longer 20, b) it wasn't really ever designed for long distance touring, and c) my Breva 1100 might have been the saner choice, its not all that bad.

Putting ergonomics aside for a while, from a mechanical standpoint, the 750 is a surprisingly good choice for long distance riding. The tall gearing which makes the bike a bit of a pig in town, translates into effortless cruising. It prefers to be in fourth at a steady 100kph (just around 4000 rpm) and starts to get positively balky in fifth at anything below about 105kph.

OK, so it doesn't have a windscreen, so riding the last 10 hours into a 60kph headwind was a bit of a nightmare. But in every other way it was a fine ride. The handling is exemplary (by any standard I have been exposed to) and it has that 'cool' factor which puts a big smile on my face even in the middle of nowhere. Is 750 enough? I should say so!

The bike wasn't really the issue I was wrestling with. I was trying, unsuccessfully I might add, to get at the root of what it is that drives me to take older bikes on torture tours to some of the more remote parts of eastern and central Canada. I'm not trying to break the bikes, honest I'm not. They are Guzzis! Remember that original design brief - able to withstand the abuses of squaddies and cops for at least 100,000 kms without major mechanical intervention. No, breaking the bikes isn't even on the cards, although I do get a wry pleasure with having to deal with whatever minor troubles do occur on the road.

Breaking myself then? Testing my mortality? There's a possibility. Perhaps I'm waiting for something to break.

I awoke at 4:30 and was on the road before 5. Morning light was just beginning to make an appearance in the eastern sky and moonlight was still shining down from the west. I had packed the bike the night before, so I turned the key, the bike sprang into life and, not wanting to irritate the neighbours more than usual, I headed down the road as quietly as possible.

I love that time of day. Most people are still in bed, so the roads are quiet and apart from the occasional skunk or deer, I have the roads to myself. I love the early morning mist, the way it hangs in the valleys and condenses on my visor. I can usually have a couple of hundred kilometres under my belt before most people have hit the snooze button.

This morning there was plenty of chilly mist in the valleys and the short ride to the highway had me reaching for my gloves and wishing for the Breva's heated grips. I joined highway 401 just east of Kingston, cranked the 750 up to a steady 110kph (fast enough to make time - no so far above the 100kph limit to attract the attention of the police) and joined the transport trucks on the early morning parade east.

After about an hour and a half I stopped for gas and coffee in Prescott. That first coffee always seems triply welcome. It appeases the raging caffeine monster inside, warms chilled hands, and triggers a gastro-colic reflex.

I try and organize my food breaks with gas stops. For me, a perfect stop is the village gas bar / grocery store / liquor store where I can grab all the necessities for the day without having to spend any time waiting, queuing or looking at menus. Stopping for gas is unavoidable and I resent it. Stopping for food and drink can be delayed. The booze is for later.

I crossed from Ontario into Quebec at Salaberry de Valleyfield a sprawling town on a large island in the St. Lawrence River. Rather than struggle through the urban nightmare of Montreal, I chose a southern loop around the city, passing through the small towns of Sainte Hyacinthe and Yamaska before re-crossing the St. Lawrence at Sorel-Tracy, about 80 kilometres downstream from Montreal.

On a typical trip day, I'm pretty much on the bike from dawn till dusk and this day was to be no exception. I wasn't interested in sight-seeing so I droned along on Highway 40 past Quebec City, re-entering the atmosphere of two-lane traffic just west of Beauport. It had been playing on my nerves that although I had my tyre irons and a puncture kit with me, I had neither spare tube nor pump. On impulse I pulled into a Suzuki dealer and with plenty of gestures and some Franglais, managed to communicate my need for a tube to the helpful sales guy. The only 18inch tube he had in stock was a motocross tube - better than nothing, I thought.

Because I'm an old geezer on an old bike, I usually find myself travelling slightly slower than the ambient speed on Quebec highways (posted speed 100kph, my speed 105-110, ambient speed 115+). Most vehicles just breeze by: back-seat kids noses pressed to the window, parents stoically or disinterestedly looking forward. Occasionally someone will pull along side for a while and I get the full fledged, appreciative, enthusiasts thumbs-up.

A couple of years ago, as the last leg of a father-son three day blast, my eldest son Sam (on his VFR) and I (on my Breva) had put in a long day riding from Tadoussac to home, virtually in rain the whole way. I was determined to beat our record, so set my sights on Forestville, a village another 100 kilometres down the valley.

By the time I got there, I was tired and sore, but pleased with the bike and with myself. A bottle of cheap red wine, some chips, a motel room with the Olympics on the TV and a classic bike outside - its hard to imagine a better life.

Although I was back on the road before 6AM, both my head and the atmosphere were a bit fuzzy. Almost immediately I swung into the McDonald's parking lot, thinking of grabbing a coffee before settling in to the next leg, but the smell of grease so early in the morning didn't sit well, so I swung out again just as quickly. A thick, damp morning mist had settled in off the river so the stretch between Forestville and Baie-Comeau passed in a bit of a blur, both literally and figuratively. I had to keep wiping my visor with the back of my gloves so that my view of the road ahead didn't stop an inch in front of my eyes.

Baie Comeau is a small industrial town on the St. Lawrence River, rather vaingloriously described on its official web site thus:

"As the voluminous waves of the St. Lawrence unfurl at its feet, Baie-Comeau, daughter of forests and sea, beckons to the world beyond its port. As soon as you set foot here, the river's constant presence will imprint a lasting memory on your senses, and the lure to traverse its waters to see marine mammals and wild ducks won't subside until you give in to it."

Well! The only thing most Canadians know about Baie Comeau is that it is the home town of one of Canada's least-loved Prime Ministers - the Right Honourable Brian Mulroney, who, after two terms in office, led the Progressive Conservative Party to a stunning collapse. The oldest political party in Canada was reduced from a 151-seat majority to two seats in the worst defeat ever suffered for a governing party at the federal level.

I mainly know it as the place you turn left towards Labrador City, so from Baie Comeau onwards was Terra incognita for me. And I was impressed. Almost as soon as you leave the built up area, there are high wooded slopes, cliff faces, hanging lakes and stunning views of the river below. Uncharacteristically, and despite the lingering residue of the morning mist (both kinds), I stopped at an official viewing platform to take in the view towards Anse Saint-Pancrase. A well maintained board walk overlooks a dramatic, glacially sculpted defile leading down to the river. It was blessedly empty of other gorpers and the view was worth the stop.

The road continues to hug the coast virtually all the way to Sept Iles - heck, for that matter it hugs the coast all the way to Natashquan, never veering more than a few kilometres inland, usually to cut across a headland or avoid a particularly truculent lump of pre-Cambrian hillside.

High 138, north east of Baie Comeau

As I rode along, with the road almost magically to myself most of the time, I had been going through my inventory of tools and supplies in my head. I realised that although I had bought a new tube, I still had no way to inflate it, and perhaps, more uselessly, I had forgotten to bring a wrench that would fit the wheel nuts. Fortunately, like the ubiquitous Tim Horton's, even relatively small towns have a Canadian Tire - Canada's basic utility / automotive / hardware store, and Sept Ilse was no exception. I walked out with a sizeable adjustable spanner, a $9 bicycle pump, two packets of ear plugs and a pair of clear safety goggles.

Beyond Sept Ilse, the dramatic 'old mountain' scenery where the Canadian Shield meets the valley gives way to a broad coastal sand plain. The hills can still be seen, but they are well back from the current shore. In times past, when the weight of glacial ice had depressed this part of the continent and before it had rebounded (isostatic rebound), the St. Lawrence would have been a much wider valley in this area, so effectively I was riding along on part of the old river bed.

By mid afternoon, I was still going well. I had stopped a few times to gas up or take a few pictures, and each time had noticed an unusual, but slight low speed shaking in the steering when I pulled away - but for the most part I was well settled in, the bike was running well and I was making distance. I breezed past Havre Saint Pierre having decided that the end point at Natashquan was definitely within reach if I was prepared for a longish day.

There is an official rest area just past Havre Saint Pierre. These rest stops usually offer a scenic view and I had often used them. So far I had ridden about 560 kilometres so it was time for a snack anyway. This time, as I pulled to a stop I could feel that something was definitely wrong. The steering was dull and shaky. Damn - my front tyre was flat!

Unscheduled stop near Havre Saint Pierre

It could have been worse. I had a puncture kit, a pump, a nice view, tools, no bugs, nice weather, a picnic bench for my gear and a hard surface for the centre stand. I set to work. Damn - I'd forgotten that the front axle has Allen key pinch bolts and I didn't have an Allen key that large. As luck would have it, the pinch bolts weren't too tight, so with a bit of gentle bashing and hammering, I was able to remove the axle and then the wheel. Finding the puncture was easy - just a small hole - so I opted to try a fix rather than install the new tube.

A truck full of road crew guys turned up to empty the garbage containers, and of course, were captivated by my dilemma. One fellow, who had a few words of English, communicated that there was a tyre repair shop in Havre Saint Pierre and made it clear that they would help me somehow if I needed it. I indicated that I was fine.

"Where are you from?" I answered that I was from Kingston, Ontario.
"Do you know Linda? I used to visit her there twenty years ago......"

Sometimes I surprise myself with rarely executed bouts of common sense. I rode the short distance back to Havre Saint Pierre, added some more air to the tyre at the gas station, then headed for a motel. Predictably, in the morning the tyre was as flat as a pancake!

Whether it was because I had been feeling a bit raunchy the previous morning, or perhaps because of an uncharacteristic moment of restraint, I hadn't enjoyed my traditional 'on the road' suppertime beverage, so I was feeling fresh as a daisy until I looked out of the window and saw the flat.

5AM isn't really a civilized time to start changing a tube, but I did my best to keep the clanking of tyre irons to a minimum and because I'd had practice the previous day, I managed to get it changed and the wheel back on the bike within half an hour. Stuffing the heavy motocross tube in the skinny 3.5 x 18 tyre was a bit of a struggle, but it went in, and more to the point, held air. I put a few pounds in with the hand pump, then slowly rode to the nearby garage where, fortunately, their air line was still working.

Its only 108 kilometres from Havre Saint Pierre to Natashquan and I took my time. Firstly I had forgotten to gas-up in H-S-P so had to take it easy until I could find somewhere open, and secondly, the scenery had changed. The pre-Cambrian hills and sand plain forests had been left behind. I had now reached the sub-Arctic zone. When traveling Highway 138, its easy to be deluded into thinking you are traveling east - after all, you are heading towards the Atlantic from the centre of the continent. In fact, you are travelling northeast at almost 45 degrees to the equator. Its not far north in absolute terms, since you only cross the 50th parallel on the way - about level with Cornwall in the UK - but environmentally and climatically, you are getting up there.

And to provide a sense of scale, when flying to Europe from Toronto, you spend more time flying up the St. Lawrence River Valley than you do over the open Atlantic Ocean!

For some inexplicable reason, I have a fascination with the world of muskeg, bog, low, glacially ground rocky hummocks, little trees, spruce bog, caribou moss and moose pasture. To some, it must seem like the least engaging environment on the planet. It is flattish, open, wind blown, desolate, almost devoid of signs of life - and I love it. Riding along through this wild, low, open empty landscape thrills me. You can tell that the ice sheets only left the day before yesterday. It cares nothing for your life or death. God walks there in silent contemplation every day.

I had to hang around in the village of Baie Johann-Beetz (population 81) for half an hour until the gas station / grocery store opened at 8AM. I didn't mind - its beautiful. A gorgeous salmon stream bisects the village, flowing over glacially smoothed granite on its way to join the St. Lawrence. I clambered around on the rocks for a while taking pictures before making my way back to where I had parked the bike at the gas bar. Right on time, a young lady arrived to open the shop and switch on the pumps. I filled up, bought some granola bars, shared a laugh over the fact that neither one of us could understand a single word the other was saying, and headed towards Natashquan.

The last few kilometres to Natashquan are narrow, rough, twisty and would have been enjoyable had it not been for the roadworks in progress along this stretch of the highway. In remote areas, Quebec uses automated traffic lights with a digital display counting down the seconds you have to wait until the light changes. The first one I encountered was counting down at 139, so I had plenty of time to get off the bike, adjust my gear and stretch my legs before it got to zero and green.

Natashquan is two distinct and separate communities. The smaller French-Canadian village of Natashquan (pop 246) is a neat little community straddling the mouth of the Petit Natashquan River. The First Nations Innu village of Natashquan (pop 810) lies at the mouth of the much larger Natashquan River. Only 1.9% of its inhabitants list French as their first language!

The paved portion of Highway 138 ends just east of the Innu village of Natashquan. Frankly, it's a bit anticlimactic. You turn the corner past the reserve, and there is the sign indicating the end of the road. A gravel road actually continues for another 18 kilometres along the river, but I had been bullied in to swearing I wouldn't abuse the 750S with extensive gravel riding.

After his first ride on the 750S, my son Sam claimed it as part of his inheritance (mind you, I don't know what he imagines the rest might be!)

and, knowing me well, made me promise I wouldn't beat it to death along rough gravel roads. Grudgingly I accepted his request, and to honour that, I ended my trip at the end of the pavement.

It was still early in the day, so I took a few photographs, turned the bike around then headed for home. Google maps list the distance / time from Natashquan to Forestville as 697 km, 10 hours 11 mins. I don't think it took me quite that long, even with numerous stops for photographs. I will admit to being a bit tired by the end of the day though, so before heading to the same motel I'd stayed in on the way up, I filled up with gas, bought a bag of tortilla chips, a jar of cheese dip, a bottle of "La Fin du Monde (the End of the World)!" 9% alcohol beer and a can of Sapporo for supper.

I spent a happy evening watching the Olympics on TV, ingesting my disgusting suppertime fare then hit the sack. At about 1.30AM my body decided to rebel................

I like to think that the long hours in the saddle and the unremitting sunshine of the previous day had been what made me feel so grim in the middle of the night, but I fear my unwise culinary choices were really responsible. I won't bore you with the details - let's just say I had a rather sleepless night - and I was a little slower to rise and my breath was a little worse than usual in the morning. Nevertheless, I was on the road by

6, making my way towards Tadoussac and the ferry across the narrows at the mouth of the Saguenay Fjord.

The line-up for the ferry wasn't very long and the bike and I were soon aboard. The mouth of the fjord is a famous whale-watching location. I scanned the horizon and was rewarded by seeing a small pod of dolphins making their way inland.

The 750S was running beautifully, the air was still and my health (and appetite) had returned so I pressed on for another 75 kilometres and pulled in at the MacDonald's at La Malbaie.

"Bonjour", I started, to the young man behind the counter.

"Bonjour. What can I get for you Sir?"

Somewhat startled, I replied, *"How did you know - I only said one word?"*

"It was your accent........"

The coffee worked it's magic, and with a big dollop of special sauce in my belly, I felt ready for anything. I checked the map. Only another 716 kilometres to home - nothing to it.

From La Malbaie the road turns inland, rising over a series of substantial hills, up to 600 metres or more above the river. I had noticed a freshening wind when I left MacDonald's but the weather continued to be warm and a bit of a breeze was welcome on the few occasions I had to come to a stop. To say the 750S romped up the hills would be to stretch the truth. With the increasing wind, it was becoming quite a struggle to maintain the legal limit, even having to drop down to third on some of the steeper sections. Nevertheless, riding was still enjoyable, and if I was having to hold on to the bars a little more tightly than usual, that was to be expected.

I stopped briefly in a drug store parking lot in Beaupre to shed some clothes and perform a quick, preemptive spark plug swap before hitting Quebec City. I always carry a couple of spares, and now seemed as good a time as any to use them. The digital board on the wall of the drug store was reading 32 degrees centigrade.

My plan was to cross over to the south side of the river at Quebec City, follow Highway 20 then loop south around the skirts of Montreal. By carefully following the road signs for Pont Pierre Laporte, I was unwittingly guided right through the heart of Quebec City and city traffic - exactly the place I didn't want to be in this heat. As the traffic slowed and the bike heated up, the clutch started to drag. I tried a quick cable adjustment at the lever but it had no effect. Unless I snicked it into neutral before coming to a halt, the bike would stall if I let the revs drop and tug forward unless I kept the revs up. Even more annoying, the clutch was becoming like an on-off switch, making pulling away again jerky and loud. The bike and I lurched and screeched up one hill within sight of the walls of the old town, as I desperately tried to find that elusive spot between fully engaged and mostly disengaged. Fortunately traffic along Boulevard Laurier wasn't too thick and by the time I was on the slip road to the bridge, the bike was behaving itself again.

Highway 20 is a fast, straight four-lane highway that cuts straight across flat, rich farmland. The wind had increased in velocity and was gusting strongly. I swear I spent much of the next couple of hundred kilometres fighting the quartering wind while bracing for the inevitable gusts which would push the bike sideways and lay it over at what seemed like 45 degrees. The journey was starting to be wearing, both physically and psychologically. By this time I was riding in a tee-shirt. A short, sharp downpour had soaked me but failed to make a dent in the heat. I was completely dry within minutes. The wind had become so strong that the loose skin on the bottom of my upper arms was flapping so vigorously that it was painful. Despite the oppressive heat, I had to put my jacket back on.

Crossing the river again and entering Ontario beyond Salaberry de Valleyfield, the cross wind became a headwind.

To say the next few kilometres were a bit of a struggle is an understatement. In my experience, there is a point in just about every long distance ride where a combination of factors conspire to make life truly miserable. I had reached that point. Despite the sheepskin and beaded seat covers I use, the 750Ss seat had become an instrument of torture. The muscles of my neck, forearms and hands were exhausted from keeping my body from being blown off the back of the bike and my knees had decided that no matter how many times I put my feet on the rear pegs for a change of position, they had had enough.

Normally I can ride through it. My posterior is case-hardened from lots of kilometres and I seem to be able to shut out any reasonable amount of discomfort. I have found that if I set some goals such as "just another 40 kilometres then I'll take a break" that often, by the time the 40 kilometres are up, I have worked through the discomfort and am ready for more. Not this time.

As I battered my way along the highway, I found myself longing for my 830lb Yamaha 'Colossus of Roads' - the Royal Star Tour Deluxe I used to own. That bike wouldn't be blown around on the highway. That bike, with its barn door fairing wouldn't have my shoulders shrieking for mercy or my knees folded like a pretzel. That bike's clutch wouldn't have caused me problems in Quebec City. That bike's effortless power.... - heck, I could have put it in cruise control and just sat back and relaxed.............

With treacherous thoughts like these reverberating in my head, I pulled into the new 'On Route' service centre at Ingleside to gas up and give my battered body a rest. I sat inside for quite a while in air conditioned luxury, enjoying a cold drink, commiserating with a cleaning lady whose shift had only just begun, when I saw that my helmet had blown off the bike. I rushed outside before some cretin ran it over in the busy parking lot. Just as I reached the bike an elderly man turned to his wife and said,

"Now that's a proper bike. A real classic."

I got off the highway at the next exit and took a slower road, where the wind drag on my body was minimal. Riding the last few kilometres home along the St. Lawrence Parkway, the 750S burbling along contentedly beneath me, all struggle and discomfort had disappeared. I had reached that happy place beyond the pain.

I have no interest in making the 750S too pretty. Some of the paint is missing around the fuel filler cap but the tank isn't rusty and it doesn't leak. The chrome around the headlight shell and on the swan neck clip-ons is a bit pitted, but that's all fine with me. I have replaced the clutch - an interesting procedure involving disassembling the back end of the bike then 'crabbing' the frame in order to be able to remove the gearbox. While this involved a bit of work, the silver lining is that while you have it all apart, you can check the condition of the drive splines, carrier bearings and universal joint at the same time and lube, replace and repair as necessary. Fortunately mine were all in good condition. I also recently replaced the original ignition switch which had become erratic and a bit dangerous as it would start to crank the engine in virtually any key position. Even though my bike can best be described as a '1972/4 mostly 750S' and is an amalgam of parts, not a 'pure' - as the factory intended - model, it exhibits almost all of the characteristics of what many people consider to be Moto Guzzi's most aesthetically pleasing motorcycle. I'm told that even with its unusual heritage, it is still a bit of a collector's item and worth much more than I have invested in it. For me though, any value the bike has, comes from bringing it back in to reliable, road-going condition. I was extremely lucky that there was such a good, barely used core to work from so getting it road-ready wasn't too arduous. In my opinion, bikes like the Moto Guzzi 750S were not built to be tarted and cosseted. They were designed to be ridden far and hard.

THE JAMES BAY ROAD DEBACLE

This is a sorry tale of personal incompetence, good fortune, endurance, isolation and the kindness of strangers. Let me set the scene. This time, I decided it was time to tackle the Trans-Taiga Road - a 600+ kilometre gravel road into the centre of northern Quebec. 40 year old bike, aged rider, thousands of kilometres of virtually unserviced empty road in the middle of bear, wolf and blackfly infested wilderness - what could possibly go wrong?

The Trans-Taiga Road branches east from the James Bay Road about 80 kilometres south of Radisson, but to get there you first have to ride most of the James Bay Road. I won't bore you with the technical details here, but let's just say, it's a long way.

My journey started just north of Kingston, Ontario, through Perth and Calabogie, crossing the Ottawa River into Quebec at Portage du Fort, just north of Renfrew. From there, it's a pleasant ride through the wooded hills and lakes of the Pontiac District to Maniwaki.

As always, at the start of one of these journeys, I'm tuned in to the bike, listening for any rattles or knocks which might spell trouble. I had adjusted the valves the night before I left, and if the ticking from the upper end of the motor sounded a trifle louder than usual, I put it down to the generous clearances stipulated in the manual. Old Guzzis have loud valves - that's just the way it is when your jugs are hanging out in the air on either side of the gas tank. I like to hear them while I'm riding - like the constant chirping of crickets. As long as you can hear that mechanical cacophony, all is right in the world. What I didn't know at that time was that the slightly heightened chirping was caused by a loose generator mount, adding its own vibratory message to the chorus.

Beyond Maniwaki you join Quebec Highway 117 heading through the *Reserve faunique La Vérendrye* (La Vérendrye Park) for the best part of 250 kilometres until the town of Val D'Or. This is the most scenic portion of the journey, the road winds between granite hills, past massive lakes and moose pasture. Although it is a well traveled, nicely paved route, there are few services and one starts to get a sense of the vastness of Quebec.

The Eldorado was running well, maintaining a steady 60mph (indicated 70, courtesy Veglia Instruments) at a comfortable 3500 rpm. Other than stopping occasionally to add fuel or check the oil, it was just a case of droning along in the sunshine. I like droning. It becomes a meditative state where the lizard brain takes over the mundane stuff of keeping the bike between the gravel shoulder and the centre line, while the other parts go off to some other place. Don't ask me what I think about on long rides - everything, and nothing. I spent the first night in Amos, settling down in a motel with a few beers and some nasty orange corn chips - the kind that old married guys like to indulge themselves with when they are out of reach of their more health conscious spouses.

Its about 200 kilometres between Amos and Matagami and the start of the James Bay Road. I've ridden that stretch before, but for some reason this time it seemed interminable and I just wasn't reaching my 'Zen' state. The kilometre marker posts seemed to crawl by and time itself seemed to have slowed down. You would think that 200 kilometres of road flanked by forest extending endlessly to either side would give one a sense of being 'out there', but the real ride doesn't start until you are

It's a long way to anywhere.

past Matagami. The little town is about a kilometre off the main road, but bypass it at your peril - the next fuel pump (and little else), is 381 kilometres to the north.

Needless to say, I topped off with gas, checked my oil, then rode the 6 kilometres to the checkpoint where you register your trip. From this point on, there are no services, only a handful of (often uninhabited) First Nations cabins, usually tucked in the forest just off the road.

I derive a perverse pleasure heading out on to an empty road. I'm not sure why. I am conscious of the dangers. Misjudge a single corner or fall asleep in the saddle and you could fly off into the bush or swamp, leaving virtually no trace that you'd gone that way. You and your bike could simply never be found. Stop, and within a few moments hoards of blackflies descend. It's not wolves and bears you have to fear out here - it's the blackflies that will tear you to pieces. The emergency phone installations only serve to remind you just how remote it is. It can be hours between vehicles.

The landscape has a subtle charm. There are no outstanding features - indeed, featurelessness is one of its defining characteristics. At first it just seems as though you are riding through an endless tunnel of trees, but the further north you go, the trees get smaller and the bones of the landscape become more apparent. Here and there a bit of bedrock or an area of bog will be visible between the stunted spruce. Occasionally you can get a glimpse of the true immensity of the landscape - it seems to roll on forever. The road is a thin line across this enormous terrain.

Apart from what was in my mostly full tank, I was carrying an extra 20 litres of gas. Contrary to expectations, the weight of the gas on the rear rack had almost no perceptible affect on the Guzzis razor sharp handling characteristics. It wallowed through the corners a fraction more, perhaps, but not enough to be worrisome. So when I reached where the Trans-Taiga Road meets the James Bay Road at mid afternoon, I had more than enough gas to make the first leg of that journey.

But I dithered. Was it a premonition or just cowardice? I rode up the road for about 200 metres. The gravel was loose and dry, but neither better nor worse than roads I have ridden hundreds of kilometres on before. I turned around and decided to have one more night of luxury in a motel in Radisson, before setting out in earnest.

Twenty kilometres later, the Eldorado was DRT (Dead Right There) at the side of the road, out of cell range, with oil gushing from a broken oil line.

I was stranded about 60 kilometres south of Radisson: pushing the bike was out of the question, so I set about preparing myself. First things first - I rooted my bug net out of my tank bag. The little bleeders (and I use that term quite accurately) had already descended and were starting to rip holes in my flesh. For those of you who haven't had the pleasure of encountering blackflies - I do not exaggerate. They land, bite a little piece of flesh invariably drawing blood, leaving their nasty toxins in the wound. Individually they are a minor irritation, but they descend in the thousands. My tank bag contained all the portable stuff, such as my cameras, phone and wallet, and I had barely pulled it off the bike when I heard a vehicle approaching.

The instant my thumb was in the air, the driver jammed on the brakes. I didn't catch the gentleman's name - let's call him Pierre - but Pierre had instantly read the signals, and, well, you just can't go past someone in distress on these roads. Within moments I was in the cab, negotiating a mutually intelligible language, and we were back up to Pierre's normal cruising speed of 140+kph. We settled on English, since my French only extends to a few words, whereas despite his protestations to the contrary, Pierre's English was fully functional. I could tell it was going to be a terrifying journey in either official language.

One thing you have to understand about the James Bay Road is the frost heaves. It was well built 30 years ago but has received little attention since. Every so often, very often, there are enormous frost heaves which extend right across the road and rise abruptly up to 6 inches or more from the surrounding pavement. Ironically they are relatively easy to manage on a bike but transport trucks, and as I was to find out, pickup trucks, are thrown around vigorously. And of course, the heaves always seem to be worst on the bends, especially when Pierre's truck was already almost on two wheels and he was fiddling with his darn cell phone trying to find some reception. He must have been in control, but there were plenty of times I imagined us barrel rolling into the muskeg as the truck shook like a dog with a rat.

By the time we reached the edge of Radisson, Pierre had found a signal, called the local garage and we had been instructed to call CAA (Canadian Automobile Association), who would then call them back and authorize a tow truck. I had barely finished talking to CAA as we pulled in to the garage. It doesn't take long to cover 60 kilometres when there is zero traffic and a maniac at the wheel. The folks at the garage were equally helpful. Within a few minutes I had met my driver, let's call him Etienne, pulled myself into the cab of the flatbed, and was heading back up the road. I had been worried about leaving my bike at the side of the road but I needn't have - it was untouched on our return. Etienne and I loaded the bike, strapping it down with some monster straps. I'd thought the journey in Pierre's truck had been bumpy, but it was nothing compared to the shaking and pounding we endured in the tow truck. Fortunately the bike didn't move an inch. It was as if it was welded to the bed.

Once I'd checked in to the motel, I set about stripping the bike. If there's one thing I am reasonably smart about, its making sure I have all the tools necessary to do most stuff on the road. I know which wrenches I need for each part of the disassembly and have become quite quick at it. With the tank and seat removed, the problem was obvious: the generator had been able to vibrate enough that a) the front stay had snapped, and b) the mounting bracket had been touching the oil line where it passes though a hole in the bracket. It had partially worn through the line, but more importantly, had been vibrating against it, causing the pipe to crack.

Here's the confession part - I knew when I installed the alternator (replacing the original generator) I had done a lousy job of securing the main bolts that hold the bracket to the motor. Over the years the threads had become worn and were subject to loosening (the same had happened on the Trans-Labrador trip). I just hadn't done a proper, permanent fix when I had replaced the generator with the alternator. Mea Culpa! Will I never learn that half measures don't work? Now, what to do about the split pipe? No Guzzi dealer in Radisson! I know - what about JB Weld?

As Pierre had humorously informed me, Radisson doesn't have a Walmart, a Home Hardware, a MacDonalds or much of anything else for that matter. It's a Hydro Quebec company town with limited services and facilities. Imagine my shock then, when I found a hardware section (about 5 feet wide) in the general store and there, hanging on the panel, was JB Weld. I overcame my natural parsimony when I saw that the asking price was $15.99, with my unfounded conviction that here, indeed, could be the solution to my dilemma. Never mind that I have never once managed to do a successful JB Weld repair to anything - I guess I'm just serially optimistic. This time, I counseled myself, I will actually follow the instructions on the package, and do it right! The alternatives didn't even bear considering.

Back at the motel, I cleaned the oil from the fractured line by dunking it the gas container on the back of the bike. I gave it a moment to dry off then went inside. By carefully reading the instructions, I learned that multiple thin coats are best, and that curing time could be accelerated with heat. It was 9pm. when I applied the first coat then hung it below the bathroom light fixture to cure. I applied a second coat at 3am. giving it a bit of encouragement with a hair dryer before hanging it up again.

The metal pipe was encouragingly warm when I checked it in the morning and the JB Weld I had applied had become dry and was no longer tacky. Still, not wanting to rush anything, I went for breakfast where my pathetic attempts to order oeufs and jambon were interpreted as eggs with jam-on until we got the language thing sorted out again.

I had noticed that the garage carried a few bits of automotive hardware so thought I would see what I could substitute for the broken front bracket. I also needed some oil to replace the stuff I'd spilled all over my pristine engine cases. The fellow behind the counter, I didn't get his name so let's call him Jacques, said that he didn't have anything that would work, but perhaps his mechanic could make a replica? It turned out that his mechanic was Etienne - the flatbed driver - who was also his dad! I love the way small towns work.

It took Etienne less than half an hour to re-manufacture the bracket and I walked out of there clutching my new Guzzi part and three litres of 20/50. Life is good.

Back at the motel, the motelier (what do you actually call someone that runs a motel?) said that there was no need for me to rush the bike or to vacate the room - she wasn't in any hurry. I double checked the oil line and carefully reassembled everything before gingerly starting the bike. My Eldo has a gloriously slow and regular idle, so I let it burble away while I looked for any signs of leakage. Damn. Almost immediately oil started pouring out, not from the 'fix', but from the banjo bolt on the right cylinder head which I had forgotten to tighten properly. OK, let's try again.

This time the bike started, with no signs of oil escaping from unwarranted locations. Even the worn out alternator belt (the shaking of the alternator had ground off all the rubber blocks) was doing its job. I left it to idle while I assembled my gear and put my tools away so that all the metal parts could get nice and warm. Still no leaks - could this be possible?

I was packed and heading out of town by mid-day. I expected to feel the discouragingly warm feel of hot oil on my feet and legs at any moment. A kilometre out of town I stopped and had a good look. So far so good - no leaking or spurting fluids.

As time went by, my speed and confidence gradually increased. I passed the spot where I had been stranded then pulled to a stop at the junction of the Trans-Taiga Road. Was I daft? Not this time! To head down 600+ kilometres of unserviced gravel road with a bike whose vital fluids were held in with epoxy metal and whose alternator belt was hanging on by a thread was simply asking for trouble. I headed south.

Its 620 kilometres from Radisson to Matagami. To my astonishment, I made it to Matagami that evening without further trouble. I checked in to the overpriced motel and celebrated with half a dozen Rickard's Dark and the obligatory Doritos.

I was up and on the road before 6 the next morning. From Matagami to home is quite a haul. For starters, there's the 200 kms between Matagami and Amos, then add to that the total distance of my first day - so a total of 866 kilometres. Whether its canoeing, hiking or bike riding, I always find that by the third day I'm in the groove. My mind has begun to shut out the bum soreness that long distances inevitably create, my neck and hand muscles have just about given up bothering to scream about being held in one position for so long.

I was definitely 'in the groove' coming south through La Vérendrye Park - so much so that I completely missed the turn-off to Maniwaki and had travelled an extra 30 kilometres through Mont-Laurier before I noticed that I no longer recognised where I was. Rather than face the grotesque prospect of driving through Gatineau (formerly Hull) and Ottawa, I opted to retrace my steps until I hit a road which would link me up with my original route. Damn - an extra 60 kilometres added to my day through sheer inattentiveness. I should also mention that all was not exactly peachy with the Eldorado. The re-manufactured stay had fractured in exactly the same spot as the original so I was in a constant state of worry that the bracket might start eating its way through the oil line again. To prevent that from happening, I now had the alternator clamped down with a rat's nest of nylon webbing and zip ties. It wasn't pretty, but at least it kept the critical parts from destroying themselves.

Back in Ontario, safely across the Ottawa river, I stopped briefly in Calabogie to empty my remaining 10 litre jug into the gas tank and check my oil. As I was crouched next to the bike in a public park, a fellow on a Harley saw me, stopped, turned around and came to see whether I needed assistance. I thanked him for stopping and after a brief chat - during which he looked increasingly disturbed at the condition of my bike - he rode away. I think he may have been even more disturbed when I blasted past him a few kilometres later. He was out for a nice evening ride - I was hurrying home and had the bit between my teeth.

The final chapter in this minuscule, 4 day saga occurred within a few kilometres of home. I had been tailing a jeep along the road south from Westport. He wasn't going quite fast enough for my taste, there were few suitable opportunities to pass, and something about the way he was driving - some intangible - really annoyed me. Once I get the chance, I'll show him, I thought. Finally, just past Loughborough Lake I was able to gun by him, only to have the bike suddenly die.

Despite all the oil line and alternator troubles, the old Eldorado had plugged along flawlessly, never missing a single beat during over 3000 kilometres of steady flogging, with daytime temperatures reaching 30 degrees C. Now, she just quit - almost precisely as my friend Norm arrived in the other direction on his Suzuki Burgman scooter. Norm and I chatted for a couple of seconds then I tried the starter. The old girl just fired up as though nothing had ever been the problem and continued to run perfectly the rest of the way home.

Personally, I think she was chiding me for being a show-off. Its as if she was saying "No matter what, I'll get you home - but not if you behave like an ass!"

.....AND I ONLY SAW THREE BEARS

There are a couple of northern Ontario back roads which had been calling to me for quite a while. I have driven them in the distant past, when I used to do canoe survey work. Some time ago the idea lodged in my mind that I would like to explore them by bike. In particular, I wanted to ride in to Biscotasing - a tiny railway community at the end of the road, made famous as one of the stomping grounds of Grey Owl (Archie Belaney), in order to scope out the facilities and parking arrangements for a lengthy canoe trip I had been planning. Then from Bisco, I wanted to head over to Sultan - then perhaps down the Chapleau Highway. What better than to take the old Eldorado out for a spin, extend a weekend and accumulate some serious gravel miles. Characteristically, things didn't work out quite as I had planned. The route was approximately 1752 kilometres (1088 miles) of which a big chunk in the middle were entirely unpaved.

The journey from my place up to North Bay then Lavigne is one I have driven and ridden innumerable times. It's a nice ride but my mind was other things. I dropped in for quick beer and pizza at the Lavigne Tavern, just west of North Bay. Lavigne Tavern has hosted the annual Ontario Moto Guzzi Riders get together for a few years now and since the beers from the local craft "Highlander" brewery are most excellent, and so it the pizza, a few extra kilometres didn't seem misplaced.

From Lavingne (pronounced La-Ving!), I headed west and north past Sudbury towards Gogama. The Sultan Industrial Road (a logging haul road) was my first objective. It is a well maintained gravel road, which means a loose gravel surface on hardpack. Its OK in a truck but a bit tricky on a bike. Before too long a much smaller road cuts south towards Biscotasing - bumpy and full of potholes and wash outs - it's much more my style.

I saw the first bear on this road. He was a young fellow, about the same size as a Newfoundland dog. He had probably been booted by his mum this spring and was out on his own looking for something to eat. As soon as he saw me, he took off into the bush in a hurry.

When I arrived in Biscotasing the owner of the store was out on his balcony drinking coffee.

"Did you ride that thing all the way here?" he asked. I said I did.

"That's only the second road bike I have ever seen in here".

Along the road to Biscotasing

Biscotasing

BEYOND THE COFFEE SHOP

Apparently they see dirt bikes from time to time, but not elegant gentlemen on Italian steeds of distinction. I soon attracted quite a crowd (4), approximately 20% of the year-round population.

Just a couple of kilometres outside Bisco, I came across Herman, sitting with his 4 wheeler and trailer. He waved me down. His machine was broken - something to do with a recent, unsuccessful valve job - could I go back in to town to get his brother? You bet! Back in town I found the 'white house with the red truck' (I didn't have to look too hard), and explained Herman's predicament to his brother, who assured me he would be along with his other 4 wheeler to get him soon.

Back on the road, I conveyed this to Herman then carried on. It's a mere 32 kilometres from Bisco to Ramsey, back-tracking up the Bisco road for most of the way. On the way in I had stopped a couple of times to sit and listen.

There is a quality of silence in the northern woods that must be experienced to be appreciated. Other than the evocative call of the Canada Warbler there is nothing but the gentle rustling of the trees. Grey Owl put it best:

"........a land of shadows and hidden trails, lost rivers and unknown lakes, a region of soft footed creatures going their noiselesss ways over the carpet of moss, and there is silence, intense, absolute and all-embracing. It is as though one walked on the bottom of a mighty ocean of silence, listening, waiting for some sound which must eventually break it. " (The Falls of Silence: Country Life 1929).

Grey Owl would not be impressed by what has happened in the region since his death. His stately pines have all been cut down, massive clear cuts are everywhere and his 'hidden trails' are now a network of logging and skid roads. Indeed, he would hardly recognise the bush at all since the original forest has long since been cleared and most of what one sees is second or third growth. Fortunately nature is unremitting in her efforts to recover from our destruction. Clear cut areas rapidly bloom with spindly new growth as nature reclaims the forest. It is not the same, but at least the scars are healed over fairly quickly.

Ramsey is now a ghost town - just a small node on the trans-continental Canadian Pacific main line. In its former glory, it had a population of about 300 gold mine workers, then it was a lumber town with its own sawmill. In the early eighties, I remember seeing enormous piles of logs stockpiled along the rail tracks. Now it is deserted. The buildings have all been demolished. All that is left is a broad, bare plain which, because of the scale of the past industrial activity, nature has failed to reclaim.

As I rode out of the edge of the forest and in to the open, another teenage bear took one look at me and galloped off into the edge of the trees. He was mostly black, like most of the bears in the area, but with an endearingly cute cinnamon left ear. Unfortunately I did not have my video camera rolling at the time, so you'll just have to take my word.

My original plan had been to carry on from Ramsey to the megalopolis of Sultan but things didn't work out that way. Ramsey was so changed from what I remember that instead of turning north-west, I ended up bearing south. It wasn't until I had already covered 40 or 50 kilometres with no Sultan in sight that I realised my mistake. Oh well, I still had plenty of gas, the bike was running well and it was only about 168 kilometres from Ramsey to Webbwood along a completely uninhabited, unserviced, poorly maintained gravel road on a Sunday. Nothing to worry about..........

It was about this time that I started to notice a few problems with the road. I would be humming along, and usually about three seconds too late, would see a desultory bit of flagging tape in a bush at the edge of the road or a bit of spruce tree sitting in the middle. As I soon found out, these marked minor wash-outs and places where sink holes had developed in the road bed following recent storms. I hit the first wash-out hard, completely bottoming out the Eldo's forks and giving me a heck of a jolt. Time to be a bit careful....especially since there was bear shit everywhere. Along one section of road I counted about a dozen, really large piles of doo, about 100 metres apart. Clearly Bruin had been over-indulging on some vegetable matter and had voided his system at regular intervals as he ambled along the road.

Its odd how your mind plays tricks on you. Before I realised that I was heading in the wrong direction, I crossed a fairly substantial river flowing between lakes on either side. Something obviously twigged, because I remember thinking, 'that looks like 'the Chutes' - a well known starting point for canoe trips down the Mississagi River. I had used it myself when doing canoe survey decades ago. But because I didn't really believe it could be, I didn't fully recognise it.

Still, being only mostly lost has its benefits, and the scenery in the lands between the Mississagi and Spanish Rivers - the old "Mississagi Forest Preserve" of Grey Owl's time, is rather delightful.

The wash-outs were coming thick and fast now. Some were foot-deep channels right across the road. Others were braided networks where the run-off had done its best to turn the road into a new stream bed. I handled each with as much care as I could muster, although it's a testimony to the robust nature of the Eldorado that she took it in her stride and didn't try to unseat me even when I saw them too late and ended up hitting them full on. It was also slowly dawning on me that the road was eerily quiet. Usually you can count on some traffic - at least a vehicle every half an hour or so- but the only vehicle I had seen since leaving Ramsey had been a very off-roady jeep. I don't mind the quiet and I love having the road to myself, but this was starting to be unusual. Then I saw why!

Where's the road gone?

The road was completely washed out. No, it was just gone! I parked the bike and took a walk. The jeep and perhaps a couple of other 4x4's had managed to get through. The river bed was soft, loose and bouldery, but my options were a bit limited. I wasn't entirely sure I had enough gas to get back to Sultan (where I didn't think there was gas anyway) or Chapleau, which was almost certainly beyond my range. Better give it a go.

Riding across the first stretch was relatively painless. I took it really slowly, letting the Eldo's torque do the work, dodging the bigger rocks and relying on her power to get through the soft sections. The wash-out area was the best part of 100 metres wide, still with a small stream flowing across what was left of the road bed. I could see where the jeep had come down the far bank. It was steep and loose. If I managed to get up it, what would I find on the other side? Were there other washouts I would have to struggle through? Oh well - here goes.

At first I tried to ride the bank, but the rear wheel dug in to the loose gravel and a lost all traction. It's at times like this that you start to understand how much a 500 pound motorbike, loaded with camping gear really weighs. Balancing the bike with one hand, I managed to pull my helmet off and set it down. I was just getting too darn hot and I could see there was going to be a bit of a struggle ahead.

With the bike running in first gear, and after a couple of false starts where I almost lost it, I eventually managed to run the bike up the loose slope, controlling it (sort of) on the clutch and throttle. It's a good job I'm just a healthy teenager and not some ancient geezer with a 40 year old bike - it was a bit of a struggle!

Where's there's a will.........

Fortunately that turned out to be the only major wash-out. As I headed south there were a couple of patches where work crews had done a hasty repair and one place where a whole section of road had been rebuilt and a shiny new culvert installed, but otherwise, the road was fine.

Just above Webbwood you hit the hard top, then shortly after, join the Trans-Canada highway. I headed east to Espanola and a motel. Espanola is a pulp mill town. You can tell by a distinctive odour and the volume of steam emanating from the factory.

The following day I was on the road by six, heading through Sudbury and along the Ottawa River towards Pembroke. It was cool at first but it soon warmed up and ended up being the third wonderful day in a row. Just south of Pembroke the Eldorado started to misfire. One of my valve guides was a bit leaky but changing the cludged-up spark plug was a two minute roadside fix. After that, it was quiet roads, glorious weather and excellent scenery all the way home.

I like my Eldorado. She's a fine bike. Robust, capable, economical, solid, fast enough, easy to fix, emotionally satisfying. To others she may look a bit messy but she gets the job done.

TO SEE A PANTHER

A few weeks later, I was back up in the same area to see if I could track down some exotics. Panthers have recently made a comeback in Ontario - but sightings are extremely rare. My Eldorado was running beautifully, the weather was wonderful and there were very few bugs. I began to wonder whether this trip would just end up being a boring lap around the north-east. In the immortal words of Marriot Edgar:

"there were no shipwrecks and nobody drownded, in fact nothing to laff at at all!" (http://monologues.co.uk/Albert_and_the_Lion.htm), but the road to Eldo-love never seems to run completely smoothly and this trip was no exception.

I followed my normal route up through eastern Ontario to the Ottawa River, turning north at Mattawa, then crossing over into Quebec to ride up the east side of Lake Timiscaming. I hadn't ridden up the east side of Lake Timiskaming before and it takes quite a while since its over 100 kilometres long. The scenery is a pleasant mixture of forested, rocky hills and outcrops mixed with fine farm land with a Gallic flair. As it was Sunday, I stocked up with some Rickards Dark before I crossed back into Ontario to spend the night in an adequate, but vastly overpriced motel in New Liskeard, watching re-runs of 'Big Bang Theory' while I waited anxiously for the arrival of the new Royal baby (yeah, right!).

I choked down a quick, ready made breakfast at the motel and was on the road by 6.45AM. This part of Ontario is unexpectedly flat, and even more unexpected, given the vicious winter climate and the latitude, is covered in massive farms. Not so long ago (ie. between 8,000 and 10,000 years ago), the whole area was covered by glacial lakes Barlow and Ojibwa - massive bodies of fresh water trapped between the Canadian Shield and the retreating ice front. After the lakes had drained the remaining sediments became the Clay Belts of northeastern Ontario and western Quebec. The growing season may be short, but the soil is very fertile. The road to Elk Lake crosses part of the Clay Belt and would have been enjoyable, had it not been for the endless road works.

Past the small town of Elk Lake you are soon back into the world of rocks, trees and water of the Canadian Shield - an environment I enjoy very much.

Thirty years ago, the road across from Elk Lake to Highway 144 through Gowganda and Shining Tree was a winding gravel track. Nowadays it is paved, but it retains much of the charm and excitement of its predecessor. It is a road of almost constant curves, swooping up and down low, rocky hills, across streams and swamps and around hills. It is not a road for speed - in some areas the road bed has sunk where the heavy trucks and the annual freeze-thaw effect on the underlying gravel road bed has collapsed or heaved the road bed - and it keeps you busy, adjusting to the constantly changing road camber and watching for logging trucks. Some of the corners have signs warning that trucks will be taking up much of the road. They are not kidding! Nevertheless, it is a wonderful road; lightly traveled, picturesque and entertaining. I'd recommend it to any motorcyclist.

At Highway 144, I stopped at the 'Watershed Car and Truck Stop' to stock up on comestibles for the road (beef jerky, granola bars, chocolate milk) and gas for the bike before heading west on the Sultan Industrial Road. This time I was determined to head straight for Sultan. No unscheduled divergences along washed out roads this time. It's eighty kilometres of well groomed gravel highway to Sultan. Unfortunately the graders were out and it was being constantly groomed, so instead of a nice hard packed surface, it was like marbles on hardboard. I took it easy, letting the front wheel skitter around as it pleased and all went well.

I was through the community of Sultan before I was really conscious of it. Beyond Sultan the road is paved and arrow straight, all the way to the intersection with the Chapleau Highway. In this part of Ontario, it's a safe bet that if the terrain is flat, you are driving along the bed of an old lake. The Sultan Road runs along the bed of Lake Sultan, another massive, and relatively short-lived pro-glacial lake which eventually drained violently down the nearby Wenebegon River.

>   ROAD MAINTENANCE BY DOMTAR INC.
>   UNDER AN INDUSTRIAL ROAD AGREEMENT
>   WITH THE M.T.O.
>
>   Sorry NO SERVICES OF ANY TYPE
>   AVAILABLE ON THIS ROAD.
>
>   SULTAN ——— 80km
>   HIGHWAY 129 ——— 115km
>   BISCOTASING ——— 72km

After a quick refreshment break at the junction of the two roads, I headed south on the Chapleau Highway (Hway 129). This is one of the quieter roads in Ontario, usually carrying less than 300 vehicles per day. The first few miles are standard northern Ontario - gently curving road passing through a seemingly endless tunnel of trees.

At the Aubrey Falls Lodge I had a nice chat with a young lady regarding my canoe shuttle plans. The lodge is run by an Ojibwa family and, like so many outfitters in the region, caters to hunters, fishermen and canoeists and offers accommodation, a small restaurant / shop and gas. No gas for me though - they were out.

At this point, Highway 129 closely follows the Mississagi River, sticking closely to its east bank for miles. Although most of the surrounding hills are rounded and forested, in some places sheer cliffs and rocky headlands add variety to the scenery. The road twists and dips with the river, providing some of the most delightful riding I have ever encountered.

Up to this point the Eldo had been running flawlessly, the weather, as you can see, was about perfect (high 60's, low 70's). I was having a good time.

I have a confession to make. I may have misled you with the title to this segment. While I did passed one startled deer on the way up from eastern Ontario, I saw no bears, no moose, and, sorry if I got you all excited, but no big cats either. There were a few squished porcupines and raccoons, rapidly turning into greasy smears on the road, but no big game. This just wasn't a very good wildlife viewing trip.

But I did see a Panther!

Over the last couple of years I had been in regular touch with Ken (who rides a 74 Eldorado combo with home built sidecar), once I found out that he was rebuilding a Phelon and Moore, Panther 120. In my youth, I had owned a couple of Panthers and they still hold an important place in my heart. If I had a 'bucket list', to see a fully restored Panther would probably be on it. To ride one again......well!

Ken had imported the Panther from the UK, but soon discovered that it needed a lot of attention to bring it to a usable condition. Fortunately he's an skilled mechanic, so over a period of months, was able to disassemble, rebuild and repair the bike to a fine, original condition.

He wheeled it out of the garage, and after a couple of kicks, it roared into life. Anyone who thinks older Moto Guzzis are a bit tractor-like really needs to ride one of these. Torque is incredible and the whole feel is totally agricultural. As it was a fresh rebuild and had only been run a few times, I only rode it gently down Ken's road for a couple of minutes, but boyhood memories came flooding back. I swear the grin on my face must have been out to my ears.

From Ken's place in Webbwood, I rode east to Espanola and once again, paid far too much for a motel room. I always carry my camping gear, but the bottom line is, I find it easier to pull out my credit card than my sleeping bag. I guess I must be getting soft.

I had intended to drop in to see Guy at the Lavigne Tavern again, but since I left Espanola shortly after 5AM, and since Lavigne was fairly close, I decided he probably wouldn't want to see me that early in the morning. Instead, I just plugged away, heading east on Highway 17, bypassing Sudbury then turning south on Highway 69 towards Huntsville.

The Eldorado had been running well, but it gradually developed an annoying stutter, periodically backfiring, particularly under light load at low revs. Suddenly she just stopped dead - the computer shut her down and displayed an error code on the dash. Just kidding - she just switched into 'limp home' mode instead. I stopped endless times, making micro-adjustments to the timing, pulling the gravel dust choked K&N filters and changing the plugs. I must have pulled over to fiddle more than a dozen times. Frustrating!

Finally, I pulled in to a small roadside park to check and clean the distributor. As I pulled the cap, the lead from the coil came away in my hand. I had recently replaced the outer leads with fresh, sexy new ones, but had been too lazy to pull the tank to get at the coil lead. Where they connected to the brass distributor insert, the copper wires inside the coil lead were completely green and rotted.

I trimmed the lead, cleaned the cap then put it back together. It would be stretching the truth to say that the bike performed flawlessly afterwards. She definitely ran better, but the belching and farting continued erratically all the way home. Clearly I need to do a thorough cleaning of the carbs and sorting of the ignition system, but as usual, we finished the journey without any real problems.

I know, I know. I led you on with talk of exotic wildlife and mechanical disaster, but the reality was, I had a pleasant, relatively traffic free, three day ride through some attractive countryside and best of all, got to ride a bike from my formative years. Fabulous!

Nick Adams

YET ANOTHER BIKE

Who knows why it is that a particular brand of motorcycle gets under your skin. That's a rhetorical question, by the way, so don't feel compelled to answer. For some reason I had become afflicted with an attraction to Moto Guzzis. Perhaps it was because they are unusual, attractive to look at, simple, robust, capable, moderately powerful etc. etc. Perhaps, after a series of good experiences, we become a bit conservative in our thinking, assuming that past experiences will foreshadow the future. In any case there were now three in my garage (I'd bought a modern 2007 Breva 1100 as my 'work' bike) while another had also been resident for a while until I sold it to Doug.

From the time that Moto Guzzi first made a motorbike in 1921 until the late 1960's when they started producing the V-twins, if you mentioned 'Guzzi' to anyone, an image of a weird, low bike, with a single horizontal cylinder and a frame made up of bits of Meccano would have sprung into their mind. They used this configuration in a variety of engine sizes in everything from their very successful racing bikes, in bikes for everyday riding, and as the power unit in the Ercole - a heavy duty, three wheeled farm truck. One of the mainstays of their production had always been making robust, single cylinder bikes for the military and the police. They were greatly favoured for their reliability, ease of maintenance and their resilience to the ham-footed and ham-fisted attentions of soldiers and police all around the Mediterranean.

The last development of this noble lineage was the 'Nuovo Falcone', a plodding, archaic, clunky, 500cc single which only diverged from the earlier bikes by having a frame made of tubes, not bolted together Meccano bits, ordinary forks and a twin leading shoe front brake. Being designed mainly for 'pool' use, they were built like a tank, looked pre-war, and were as slow as porridge. I desperately wanted one!

Nuovo Falcones were never imported into North America, so to see one advertised here is an unusual event. Imagine then, my delight and surprise to find one for sale in Montreal - a mere three hour road trip away. After a quick phone call to the owner - encouragingly called Luigi - I tore the seats out of my work van and hit the road, picking Doug up along the way.

When you go to buy a bike from a private seller, you never know what you are going to encounter. In Luigi, we found a kindred spirit. He had pulled the bike out from his garage so that we could see it in the daylight, but I couldn't help noticing that much of the remaining garage space was taken up by a well-used looking Guzzi Eldorado and sidecar.

Luigi had bought the Nuovo Falcone in Italy and had it shipped back to Canada, hoping it would be a suitable bike to ride on the local roads, but he found the high seat and low foot pegs too much of a stretch for his short legs. Riding it just didn't feel safe. The bike also had a persistent misfire which he had never managed to cure.

After Doug and I had both ridden it and decided it was going home with us, Doug, bless his boots, started negotiations well below Luigi's asking price. I wasn't sure how to begin so he just jumped in. In the end we settled on a price we could all live with, loaded the bike in the back of the van and headed home.

Loaded in the van

I should have mentioned that on the way to Montreal, my van developed a persistent squeaking from the front, driver's side wheel and a grinding on tight turns. We were fairly sure that the wheel bearing was worn out, but decided to risk the journey home anyway. Well, it was worth a try! By the time we reached Cornwall, the bearing was squealing and just as we left the City limits, the steering became erratic. I pulled over on to the shoulder of the highway, as far from the traffic as I could, and we got out to have a look. Doug was out first. He had a big grin on his face. "Take a look at this" he said. I clambered out of the passenger side door and walked to the front of the van. The driver's side wheel was tilted at a crazy angle. We had stopped just in time.

As good fortune would have it, I have breakdown coverage through the CAA (Canadian Automobile Association), so after a quick call and a surprisingly short wait, the van was loaded on the bed of a flatbed truck, complete with the bike still inside. Good fortune must really have been with me that day, because we discovered that from our breakdown point to my home was just fractionally inside the 200 kilometre 'free' recovery limit. I didn't have to pay a thing - and I even saved the cost of the gas home! The flatbed dropped the van off at my local garage where I unloaded the Nuovo Falcone and rode the short distance home.

As I had with the 750S, I started riding the Nuovo Falcone on local trips - meeting Doug and others for our regular Sunday morning breakfast- a bit of back road exploration, that sort of thing. The more I rode it, the more I wanted to ride it and the kilometres started to accumulate quickly.

1974 Moto Guzzi Nuovo Falcone — Awaiting better riding weather

Make no mistake, it is slow and clunky. With the heavy flywheel, changing gears is an acquired skill. Among Nuovo Falcone riders, the joke is that when changing from first to second gear, you pull in the clutch, let the engine revs drop while saying "Saskatchewan, Mississippi, Matagami" (or some suitable, geographically appropriate variation), select second gear, let the clutch out. This can be a bit tedious when trying to make a quick start away from the traffic lights. What am I thinking? There are no quick starts away from the traffic lights. Your grandfathers old diesel Chevy Chevette would beat it off the line. You might just get a nose ahead of a fully laden gravel truck!

It doesn't accelerate as much as it accumulates speed, but it does so in such an utterly charming manner that you soon find you forget all about wanting to go fast, you settle back into that nicely sprung solo saddle and just listen to that mellow booming coming from the ridiculously over-the-top, double silencer, and the comforting mechanical clatter from the engine.

Once I'd replaced and greased the wheel bearings, put on a new chain and added some bar-end indicators, I was ready to take the Nuovo Falcone on a real road trip.

THE SWISHA ROAD

I now know why the Italian Military were content to use such a slow bike. It's tough! It may not have speed, but it has a kind of relentless, soft power that makes going virtually anywhere a practical proposition. On paved roads, it hums along, setting its own agenda, regardless of what you try to do with the throttle. Once the pavement ends, its soft suspension and endless torque eat up trails where $20,000 'adventure' bikes would fear to go.

I left home at 5.15AM. I had packed the NF the night before, so it was just a matter of kicking it over and rolling. The first few hundred kilometres were familiar territory for me, so I stopped at all the regular haunts for fuel, coffee, leg stretches and nature breaks until I reached the bridge across the Ottawa River at Rapides des Joachims and the Swisha Road.

The Swisha Road leads to Quebec's *'Dumoine ZEC'*.
ZEC's are:

"A zone d'exploitation contrôlée (in French; acronym ZEC) is a "Controlled harvesting zone". ZECs are a system of territorial infrastructures set up in 1978 by the Government of Quebec to take over from private hunting and fishing clubs (following *Opération gestion faune*). They are non profit organizations managed by honorary administrators whose primary responsibility is to manage fishing and hunting activities and see to wildlife conservation on their respective territories." (Wikipedia).

.......which, in the common tongue, means you have to pay a small fee to use the road. Since the section of road I intended to use is 206 kilometres long and unpaved the whole way, I filled my tank and spare can with fuel, and my tank bag with consumables (cheese curds, Cheetos and Fanta - I'm a bit of a health food freak) and headed up the Chemin Dumoine which follows the Dumoine River.

The first part of the road wasn't too bad - as long as you ignore the little micro-burst which had demolished a section of shoreline trees and virtually blocked the road. Beyond the blow downs, the road was a mix of cobbles, sand, puddles, sand, more sand, cobbles and gravel. Just a typical northern Canada cottage road really. After about 25 kilometres, the road crosses the Dumoine River. From this point on, you are travelling within the ZEC, although there was no noticeable difference before or after. It's all just forest and lakes, lots of lakes and numerous small streams crossed by rustic bridges.

Packed and on the road

A mini-tornado or micro-burst had brought trees down along the river bank

The mighty Nuovo Falcone took at all in its stride, chuffing along happily. If I missed a gear (which, astonishingly sometimes happens) any old gear will do. As long as the motor's actually turning over, it will pull. The road conditions were highly variable, changing from sections of soft sand to gravel and loose cobbles, with many large puddles. There were dozens of puddles: some it was possible to skirt around the edge, some not.

Swisha Road

After 100 kilometres or so of the Chemin Dumoine, the route joins a more well developed logging road that heads generally west. The gravel surface is well maintained - for logging trucks - which means for bikes, it's a squirmy, experience of washboard, loose gravel on hardpack and soft spots. Mercifully it was free of traffic, so I could ride along wherever I could find then best line. Eventually this road spits you out at Temiskaming, at the south end of Lake Temiskaming, near the pulp and paper factory.

That night I stayed in a motel in New Liskeard. I arrived at 8PM - annoying just in time for the beer and liquor stores to be closed. Fortunately my arrival didn't coincide with the 'Biker's Reunion' which attracts the 'cruiser crowd' from all across Ontario. I don't think I could have stood the strain of being around all those real bikers. I would have been embarrassed: my Guzzi has virtually no chrome and is devoid of tassles.

On the second day I headed for Elk Lake (pop 463), then onwards to Gowganda, Shining Tree and the junction of Highway 560 and Highway 144 where I was expecting to fill up with fuel. Just before getting to the gas station, the bike started to miss. At first I ignored it, hoping it would go away, but eventually it got to the point where it would hardly get me to the top of the next hill and could only maintain a reluctant 50 kph on the flat. I pulled over. The plug looked fine, although it did look as though the bike had been running a bit lean. The points looked dirty, so I scraped them off as best I could and carried on. At first the bike ran as usual, but after a couple of kilometres it started to hiccup and burp again. This time I removed leg shield and filter box and took the float bowl off the carb. There was a bit of junk in the bowl, so I cleaned that out, blew out the main jet and put it all back together. To my delight, the bike started and ran well, and the symptoms didn't reappear - just yet.

Unscheduled stop, Chapleau Highway

The gas pumps at the 'Watershed' gas station at Highway 144 were out of action. Cars and trucks were lined up waiting, like me, unable to make the next 100kms or so to the next gas station. We had no alternative but to wait until they got the pumps back on line. Fortunately, it didn't take too long and I was soon able to resume my journey - this time down the Sultan Industrial Road and another 70 kms of gravel and dust. I've ridden this road a few times on my 72 Guzzi Eldorado, and at the risk of being disloyal (and I don't think she can quite hear me), the Nuovo Falcone handles these conditions a bit better. It's not the knobbly tyres I have on the Falcone- if anything they grab the loose stuff in all the wrong places and shake the front around. No, it's probably just the difference in overall weight: the Falcone being easier to muscle around and to catch when it starts to head off line.

Towards the end of the Sultan Road, the Falcone started to hiccup again. I thought I'd fixed that problem, but no..............I stopped and fiddled, then headed south down the Chapleau Highway. Chapleau was 50 kms behind me - Thessalon, the next town was about 200 kms ahead.

In between........a single gas stop/tourist lodge.

I was still convinced that the main problem was the mucky points. Every few minutes I would have to stop and play and each time thereafter, the bike would run perfectly for about 4 kilometres then start to baulk and stutter. What was I missing? After about 150 kilometres of stop-start-splutter I'd had enough. I always carry all the necessary tools to fix just about anything at the side of the road (I may ride older bikes in the middle of nowhere, but I'm not entirely devoid of common sense), so I stopped, hauled my took kit off the back and decided I wasn't leaving until I'd fixed the problem.

First I checked the electrical system. All seemed fine. Spark good, points gapped and working well. I hope the coil isn't dodgy: banish that thought. Next check carburation. I had to remove the leg shield and filter box again, but this time the whole darn carb was coming off. So..........I emptied the bowl, cleaned all the jets then a thought struck me. What about the little screen filter between the fuel line and the carb? Predictably, I'd left the most obvious thing until last.

Needless to say, it was cludged up with gunk. I gave it a quick cleaning in fresh gas, blew it out (don't you love the taste of gas in the evening?), and reassembled. Bingo! All fixed.

Once I got in cell phone range I called Ken (he of the Panther) and on the promise of bringing beer, cadged a night in his trailer. I arrived at 9.30PM, after a tiring, but enjoyable day.

The journey home was long and uneventful. The Trans-Canada Highway has posted speeds of 90kph (55mph), so of course, most people drive at least 10 above. Except me. The poor old Nuovo Falcone is happy at an indicated 80kph (actual about 77), and is comfortable at 90kph (56mph) as long as the road is dead flat and well paved. Throw in a head wind or any kind of incline and it starts to lose momentum. The maximum speed I managed, downhill with the throttle mostly open was a GPS indicated 61.2mph - a staggering 98.5kph and acres above the posted limit. No - I recorded that speed on the Sudbury by-pass officer, where the posted limit is 100kph........whew!

It sounds awful, but it's all a matter of getting your head into the right space and learning to enjoy the ride. I always move over to let other vehicles pass, even when there's a double yellow line. I'm not interested in frustrating other drivers and I'd rather not have them breathing down my neck. Between 85 and 90kph, the Nuovo Falcone is humming, with no signs of stress or discomfort. As you can see from the distances I covered, as long as you have an iron constitution, it is quite possible to put in long days on the road. Indeed, the bike did not suffer at all on those long highway miles. It dropped not a single spot of oil, always started first kick after a brief stop and never showed the slightest signs of mechanical distress.

You can try twisting the throttle to the stop but it will get you precisely nowhere. The Nuovo Falcone has the speed it's prepared to go and nothing more. Additional throttle just results in more noise with no increase in forward momentum. When it comes to hills, the NF is going to go at it's own speed. It matters little if you try to gun it on the downslope. The revs are going to drop anyway. No point changing down: just more noise and revs, but no additional speed.

My technique, which, over the miles I began to really enjoy, was to just hold the throttle steady (almost wide open, of course) and the bike would find it's optimum. At first it's a bit disconcerting to see your road speed drop.....85.....80.....75.....70.... until somewhere between 60 and 70 kph, it hits that magic place where speed no longer diminishes and forward momentum is steady. No matter how steep the hill, the NF just chugs away at what feels like about 1000 rpm, until after a suitable eternity, you breast the rise and speed gradually increases again. The darn thing is, you can tell it's happy doing it!

Its more like driving an overloaded dump truck than a 'regular' motorbike. But here's the thing (to use a Brysonism) - it's really fun! Maintaining speed becomes a challenge, helped by the NF's awesome handling. Corner coming? No need to slow down. Keep your nerve, keep your throttle hand steady, ignore the squirming from the side treads, lean right in, around you go. Hill coming? Hammer down (a relative term, of course) then try to carry the speed up the slope, just as if you were driving a big rig. It won't make a scrap of difference but it's fun trying, as long as you can ignore the jerk in the jacked up pick-up breathing down your neck. He can bloody-well wait!

On one long hill out of Mattawa, I got a friendly wave from a speed cop in a cruiser, as I chugged past at about half the posted limit. I wonder if he realised I was pinning it. On another hill I was overtaken by an old Dodge camper van towing a newish Toyota Corolla, with bikes, boat and other sundry junk strapped on board - a mobile road block if ever there was one. He sailed past me as if I was standing still.

To those of you of the speedy crowd, it must sound horrendous, but really, as long as your head is in it, its very engaging. Exciting - perhaps not, but it certainly gives one a chance to enjoy the scenery. Ironically, on the gravel logging roads, I rode quite a bit faster than I usually do on the Eldorado, and far faster than I would dare on my modern Guzzi Breva 1100.

So there we have it. My first real trip on the Nuovo Falcone. Did it put me off taking it on long trips? Not at all. On the way home I found myself thinking....now if only I could find a route across the country that didn't involve so many miles on the Trans-Canada Highway............................hmmmm!

A bridge along the Sultan Road

Nick Adams

RETURN TO THE TRANS-TAIGA ROAD

My first trip to ride the remote Trans-Taiga Road in northern Quebec ended with the Eldorado's engine oil soaking into the gravel at the side of the road. Fortunately I managed to plug the leak and get myself home, but the main purpose of the trip had been abandoned. Riding the Trans-Taiga was unfinished business.

It was a simple plan: ride a 42 year old Moto Guzzi Eldorado to the end of the most northerly road in eastern Canada, at which point we would be at the furthest point by road that one can get in North America from any public settlement (village, town etc.). Although I almost always travel alone, on this occasion I was accompanied by Norm on his KLR.

The Trans-Taiga Road runs for 666 kilometres (410 miles) from the James Bay Road, east across the centre of northern Quebec to the Caniapiscau reservoir, which is part of Quebec's huge hydro electric James Bay Project. It is a gravel road throughout its entire length.

First though, a little context. Quebec is huge. It's twice the size of Texas, six times the size of the United Kingdom and if plonked on top of the United States, would stretch from the Gulf of Mexico to the 49th Parallel. The northern part of the province has an incredibly low population density, with about 30,000 people clustered in a few coastal villages: there are more than twice that number of black bears.

Most of the terrain is low, with areas of till plain, a few low rocky hills, and vast numbers of lakes, rivers and bogs. It looks as though the Wisconsinan Ice sheet left the day before yesterday. In geological terms, it did. The trees are stunted and sparse: 'taiga' is the sub-arctic interface between the Boreal Forest and the true Arctic.

To get to the Trans-Taiga Road, you ride up the James Bay Road - itself an isolated and uninhabited 620 kilometre (388 mile) highway. It is fully paved the whole way. I've described that road before so I won't bore you with much about it here. Suffice it to say that by the time you have reached where the Trans-Taiga leaves the James Bay Road, you are 1600kms (1000 miles) north of Toronto. It's a long way!

Norm and I met as agreed on Sunday morning at 6:30. As he rode up, I thought his KLR was vastly overloaded.

"What on earth have you got in there?" I asked, looking at his bulging plastic panniers and top box and bags strapped all over.

"Oh, just a few things......".

I suspect the all-up weight of our bikes was about the same, even though unladen, the KLR is about 150lbs lighter than the Eldorado.

The first day rolled by uneventfully. We stopped a few times for all the normal reasons: for nature breaks, to eat, to buy fuel, as well as for some sight-seeing, leg stretching and minor adjustments, but mostly, we hummed along on empty highways until we reached Matagami, 821 kilometres (510 miles) later. Norm likes to be in bed before the sun goes down, so after polishing off a few beers, we both hit the sack.

The James Bay Road starts at Matagami and ends at the small village of Radisson. 381 kilometres to the north there is a gas pump, cafeteria and some rudimentary lodging. That's it! In between there are no communities, no shops, no gas stations. Your credit card and cell phone won't help you here. If you don't have it with you, you don't have it. There are a few First Nations camps in the bush, but these are only occupied from time to time and there are no permanent dwellings. There are a few emergency phones along the route but they are intended for real emergencies. I imagine you would get a frosty (and expensive) reception if you called saying you'd run out of gas or you'd forgotten to bring kleenex. You must carry enough gas to make it to 381 so it's best to fill up in Matagami before setting out. The kind folks at the Quebec government registration building at kilometre 6 will check to see if you are adequately prepared.

I know for a fact that my Eldorado will travel 376 kilometres from completely full to completely empty. Last time I rode the James Bay Road I had filled up in Mattagami but hadn't noticed that the tap for my reserve supply was open, so instead of leaving me with about 60 kilometres of reserve fuel when the main tank ran out, I managed to drain the tank dry. Fortunately, on trips like this I always carry a plastic jug with extra fuel so I just emptied it into my tank and carried on to the gas station. This time, getting to 381 was just the beginning. There were places ahead where we needed even greater range.

By the time we reached 381, we had been traveling through burned land for more than an hour. It took at least another hour beyond 381 to get back to country that hadn't been completely devastated by fire. It didn't matter how far one could look in any direction all was burned and blackened. Forest fires are a natural part of the cycle in the Boreal Forest and this far north, no attempt is made to extinguish or control the fires. Somehow 381 had been saved, but all else was devastation. One can only imagine the toll on wildlife.

Along the James Bay Road one crosses the Rupert and Eastmain Rivers, now sadly diminished by having their natural flow diverted so that Quebec can sell power to New York. It's too high a price - turn your darn lights out! Most of the time though, you are just barrelling along between the trees, maintaining a steady speed while watching for the innumerable, 6 inch high frost heaves or 6 inch deep gullies where the roadbed has subsided. Although there is a nominal 100kph (60mph) speed limit the likelihood of encountering the police is incredibly low and some people like to take the opportunity to speed. Realistically, even riding at the limit barely gives you much of a chance to brace for the next big jolt.

At various places along the James Bay Road there are rest areas and informative signs. Unless you read French or Cree syllabics you are out of luck with the signs though. In this part of the world, the Quebecois speak French - they may have a smattering of English, but often not. The Cree speak, well, Cree, but because of their early history with English fur traders in the James Bay / Hudson's Bay area, most also speak English.

"Norm, do you have anything to clean my visor?"

"I thought you said I'd brought too much stuff", he said, handing me a cloth and a can of Pledge.

"That will cost you a beer."

Norm had been happy to ride behind me so that when I wanted to stop to take pictures he could pull over as well. I tend to take quite a few pictures and what with fiddling with two GoPros video cameras and various mounts and attachments, this had the capacity to wear thin very quickly. It didn't seem to bother Norm at all. He was quite content to pull over and wait, no matter how much fussing and fiddling I was doing.

After a long, 560 kilometre (348 mile) slog up the James Bay Road, we finally reached to junction with the Trans-Taiga Road, so we stopped to spent a little time preparing ourselves for the gravel ahead. Although the surface was fairly loose and dry, it looked like just another gravel road - although admittedly quite a long one. The last time we had been able to fill up with fuel had been back at 381, so we had already eaten up another 179 kilometres (111 miles) worth of gas by the time we reached the junction. The next available gas was 358 kilometres (222 miles) to the east at the Mirage Outfitters. Apart from what I had left in the tank, I was carrying two 10 litre jugs on my rear rack and another 5 litres in the pannier. Norm was equally equipped. We were good to go.

I have become quite comfortable traveling to remote places alone. I can definitely get myself into a predicament, but so far, at least, I have always managed to extricate myself too. Having someone else along totally changes the dynamic. Whether it's true or not, one inevitably feels some sense of responsibility for their safety and well-being. You can imagine then, it has to be a fairly special person to a) want to undertake such a journey, b) want to do it with me, and c) have the experience and fortitude to do it.

Fortunately Norm has all those qualities. He's a lifetime rider and has ridden hundreds of thousands of miles all over the continent, including to the Yukon and Alaska. Furthermore he's an acknowledged mechanical guru - a person to whom people turn for help to solve the unsolvable. Apart from all that, he's an all-around good guy, and remarkably spry considering his advanced years. I didn't have any concerns about his riding skill - indeed, his level of comfort once the going got rough was way beyond mine.

On the way up the James Bay Highway we had noticed a few snow patches in the bush. Once inland on the Trans-Taiga Road, the rivers were lined with snow and ice and the large lakes were still icebound even though it was late May.

That evening, we stopped at kilometre 203 (mile 126) along the Trans-Taiga where the Municipalité de Baie-James have established a free rest area and camp site at the crossing of the Pontois River. There was nobody else around, of course (indeed, we hadn't seen a single vehicle since leaving the James Bay Road), and we spent a delightful night, lulled by the rapids beneath the bridge and the grinding ice in the river below.

We awoke to clear skies and a healthy frost. We quickly decamped and started riding. From the James Bay Highway to Mirage is 358 kilometres (222 miles) of which we had already ridden almost two thirds the previous day. The riding was fine at first, although with some serious provisos. Traffic was sparse - virtually non-existent actually. This is Hydro Quebec's road - used to service the various dams and installations along the route - it is not a public highway. Mere sightseers like us are tolerated at their discretion.

The problem for two wheelers is that the trucks all drive the same line. The inner surface of every curve quickly becomes bare and hard packed while the outer radius is loose and deep gravel. One's inclination and tendency is to choose the bare line, but there is a very real danger of meeting a truck head-on, or if you see it in time, suddenly finding yourself running too fast into the loose stuff. Fortunately other vehicles were a rare sight. For the first 100 kilometres (60 miles) or so, everything went well. From time to time I would indicate for Norm to pull over so I could take a photograph, but the rest of the time we hummed along nicely.

The only vehicle we passed that morning was a white Hydro Quebec security SUV with a young lady at the wheel. I could tell she was a bit surprised to see us (and us too for that matter), especially since I'd been crowding her side of the road around a shallow bend and had needed to quickly adjust into the loose stuff so she could speed by. I may have wobbled around a bit as the tyres squirmed on the gravel, but nothing too out-of-control. About twenty minutes later, it didn't really surprise me to see her pulling to a halt behind us with her overhead flashers going, as I was fiddling with the camera at the side of the road.

It must have been quite intimidating to engage two big, male riders in the middle of nowhere, but through extremely broken English, she managed to make it clear she was not happy to see us, was very concerned for our well-being, and had both the authority and inclination to forbid us to ride further because of the road conditions beyond LG4 (one of the dams). Norm and I had been making good progress. Although road conditions were far from perfect, we didn't see any problem as the riding was fine, so we told her we were on top of things and promised to be careful. Reluctantly, she let us proceed and wished us well, more, I suspect, because she realised that we wouldn't have enough gas to back-track unless we went on to Mirage Outfitters first.

She was right. Beyond LG4, the road surface consisted of about four inches of freshly laid and graded gravel. It was all completely loose and horrible to ride on. Those last 50 kilometres (30 miles) to Mirage were a nightmare of squirming and sliding. It's a minor miracle that neither of us came off: the road surface was demanding so much concentration, it was no longer enjoyable.

Norm has a lifetime of gravel riding under his belt, but he was no better off on his KLR than I was on the Eldorado - it was just plain nasty. Someone with more highly developed skills and an unladen bike might have found it OK but I doubt it - and I don't think different hardware would have made a scrap of difference.

Although it was only late morning by the time we reached Mirage, we were ready for a rest. The bottom line is that for us, the ride in to Mirage was enough. To carry on any further for the dubious distinction of having been to the end of the road, would have been foolhardy and dangerous. I'm usually more than foolhardy enough for most people, but on this occasion, discretion was definitely the better part of valour.

The Mirage Outfitters caters to the kind of people who simply must travel north to kill a caribou. When its not caribou season, fishermen and Cree hunters take advantage of their excellent facilities and hospitality. They have a French chef! Food and accommodation are not cheap - but worth it.

On their way back from goose hunting, a local Cree family had shot a bear which they had lying in the back of their pick-up truck. The dad explained that this was a really important thing for them as the black bear is a sacred animal. There were important ceremonies to be performed and that virtually every part would be eaten or used. I have no objection to that kind of hunting.

While we were at Mirage we had plenty of time for some running repairs. One of the bolts holding my panniers had vibrated off. At first I thought of making a temporary fix with a zip tie, but..............

"Norm, you wouldn't have any spare nuts and bolts would you?"

"Imperial or metric? Do you need wrenches too?"

In the end we found a suitable bolt, a locking nut and some washers in his traveling hardware store.

"That will cost you a beer".

Our journey back to the James Bay Road was relatively uneventful. Despite the slippery gravel, we managed to ride the 358 kilometres without either of us falling of, although there were definitely a few 'moments'.

On the inbound journey we had noticed that my rear tyre was a bit soft. I carry a 12 volt pump but peculiarly, sometimes the tyre would inflate nicely to 25lbs - other times I could barely get it above 18. Norm thought this was a real problem while I was less concerned.

"What if you have a blow out and wreck the tyre?"

"I'll put the new tube in and run on it anyway."

He gave me one of those looks, we pumped it up again and headed for Radisson.

The James Bay Road has some long sweeping curves which we were riding at between 95 and 105 kph (59-65mph). The Eldorado waggles her a tail a bit under the best of circumstances, especially when I'm carrying a bit of fuel on the rack, but she started to feel a bit wobbly, even beyond my level of insensibility. I signed for Norm to take a look at my tyre and was given an authoritative thumbs-down. I pulled over quickly.

For some reason the pump seemed reluctant to get any air in the tyre - I assumed the pump wasn't working properly. Eventually we manage to get the pressure up to 18 pounds, but since we were almost within sight of Radisson, decided to make the last couple of kilometres.

We didn't.

Just one kilometre short of the village, the tube let go. Norm was concerned that the tyre was wrecked, but fortunately it was still fine, if worn and square from running with low pressure for so long. Within a couple of minutes we had the bike on its side, the wheel off, and the tube out. As we were close to Radisson there was a bit more traffic than we were used to. Just about every vehicle that passed either stopped to offer assistance or slowed to see whether we were all right! After a few minutes we had the new tube in and managed to get the failing pump to provide enough air to get to the village. It was an interesting end to a long hard day.

The culprit had been a two inch nail. From the way the tyre had been behaving, I'm assuming the nail had been in there all the way to Mirage and back - over 700 kilometres on the gravel, only to let go within sight of civilization. Good old girl.

After supper and a few beers, we settled in as the only campers at the municipal campground in Radisson. I think we both slept like the dead.

The last couple of days were basically a rewind of the first two: a long haul back down the James Bay Road to home. After an early breakfast, we were on the road by seven heading due south. You might think that endlessly droning down a highway lined with stunted trees, with few stunning views, no outstanding scenery and almost no other distractions would get boring. It hasn't become boring to me. The smell of the air, the sound of the motor and the unfurling of the road ahead all have their charm and anyway, you are far to busy trying to avoid having your hips jammed up between your shoulder blades as you hit yet another enormous frost heave.

As before, I stopped from time to time to take a few pictures: a few more pictures of burnt forest, another river, a Cree hunt camp, whatever caught my eye. After one such stop, I turned the key, the dash lights lit, but the starter didn't crank. Norm looked a bit worried but I leaned over, wiggled the spade fitting at the solenoid a couple of times and turned the key again. The Eldorado burst into life once more. Over the sound of her steady idle, I turned to Norm and said:

"Its one of the advantages of knowing your bike....."

He probably thought, 'pompous git', but he knew what I meant. If you've ridden enough miles on an old machine, you get to know all of her tricks. Of course in Norm's world, that dodgy electrical contact would have been found and fixed long ago and would never have given him trouble.

At another one of our stops - and I can't remember exactly how he phrased it - Norm made some comment about the low, bedrock hills being the ancient bones of the earth, exposed and scraped clean by the passage of glacial ice. Meanwhile, I was looking for an opportunity to photograph another odd phenomenon I had noticed. This recently deglaciated landscape is laced with low eskers: the beds of former rivers and streams running across the glacial ice. When the ice melted, the river bed - rocks and all - was deposited as a linear rock pile. These features often snake for miles across the landscape. The forest fire had removed all the surface vegetation and soil, leaving the river bed rocks exposed and visible.

We made it to Amos that night - another 800km (500 mile) day. After a few beers we both slept well. Even my snoring didn't keep Norm awake.

Our last day was going to be another long one. I'm a bit tall for the screen on the Eldorado so I had been suffering a bit from wind blast all week. I usually have a section of visor bolted on to deflect the air but for some reason I had left it behind. A bit of pizza box and some of Norm's industrial strength camo tape did an elegant and effective job. It's a bit 'Red Green' but it worked. I think it cost me another beer! By the time we reached the Ottawa River and the border between Quebec and Ontario, the skies had darkened with small thunder clouds. The rain was sporadic and hard, but blissfully warm. After days of endless sunshine and blue skies it was almost a relief.

A few facts and figures
    Total days = 6
    Time off at Mirage = 0.5 days
    Total distance ridden = 3988 kilometres (2478 miles)
    Total distance ridden unpaved = 716 kilometres (445 miles)
    Average vehicles encountered per kilometre (Trans-Taiga) = 0.016
    Greatest distance between sources of fuel = 537 kilometres (333 miles)
    Number of minutes ridden 'Dakar style' = 0
    Pucker moments = 62
    Most northerly Latitude reached = 53' 47
    Crashes = 0
    Breakdowns = 1
    Distance ridden with nail in tyre = more than 600 kilometres (372 miles)

FINAL THOUGHTS

While I was on the road, I did a lot of thinking about why I take old bikes on long trips, often miles from help and certainly miles from the nearest dealer. I keep a modern bike in my garage, which superficially at least, would seem to offer higher potential reliability, better suspension, more agile handling and higher levels of performance (for those long highway slogs home). But....while the modern bike is great, it just doesn't have the charm, character, class and charisma of the older bikes. I get more enjoyment from riding them, for all their warts and handicaps. I've ridden plenty of modern bikes and I'm usually bored with them within 5 minutes - they just do everything too well!

As far as being a suitable bikes for the road conditions on the Trans-Labrador Highway, the Swisha Road or the Trans-Taiga Road, I'll let the results speak for themselves. Other than problems resulting from my shoddy maintenance or my inattention to proper servicing, the bikes behaved perfectly. Old Guzzis are built like tractors, which, in my world, is a good thing. The advent of the modern 'adventure bike' has brought with it an undercurrent of suggestion that only bikes of that description are suitable for ride to out-of-the-way places. Not true! All bikes are adventure bikes - it's just a state of mind. So - if you are thinking of riding the Trans-Labrador Highway or any of Canada's more remote roads, don't think that you have to plonk down your hard-earned cash on a new 'adventure' bike. You may be more comfortable, a little safer, have less chance of a break down and a lot poorer if you do. It may be nice, but it just isn't essential. Take the bike you love, whatever that might be - then together you can have a real adventure.

As I finish compiling these short accounts of my travels, it's late January, we are deep in the annual deep freeze and the roads are covered in ice and snow. Even though the weather has been below zero for weeks and regularly dips down to -25C, that trouble-maker Doug is riding around on his bike, although even he is sensible enough to have attached a sidecar for a bit of stability. He turned up yesterday, dressed in a snowmobile suit. Although it was -10, he assured me he was perfectly warm behind his Guzzis big screen and his home-made leg shields.

My bikes are out in the garage, ready for the road and patiently waiting for a break in the weather. Sooner or later, we'll get a brief warm spell, I'll be able to dig the Eldorado out of the garage and enjoy a few more 'Stolen Days'. Until then, I'll just pray we have an early spring, look at a few maps and dream of some more adventures to distant places.

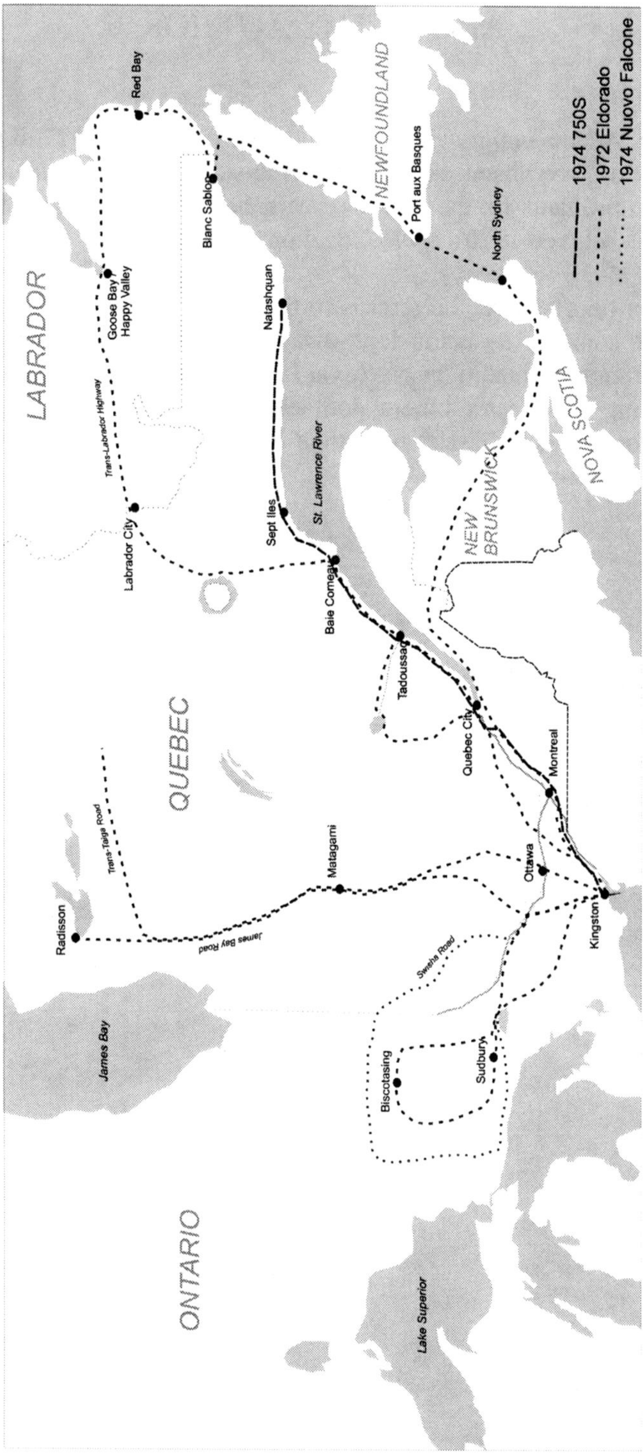
LABRADOR
QUEBEC
ONTARIO
NEWFOUNDLAND
NEW BRUNSWICK
NOVA SCOTIA
Red Bay
Blanc Sablon
Port aux Basques
North Sydney
Goose Bay
Happy Valley
Trans-Labrador Highway
Natashquan
St. Lawrence River
Sept Iles
Labrador City
Baie Comeau
Tadoussac
Quebec City
Montreal
Ottawa
Kingston
Matagami
Trans-Taiga Road
Radisson
James Bay Road
James Bay
Biscotasing
Sudbury
Lake Superior
1974 750S
1972 Eldorado
1974 Nuovo Falcone

ABOUT THE AUTHOR

Nick Adams emigrated to Canada from the UK in 1977 to work for the Ontario government as an archaeologist. He soon fell in love with Canada's north and, for the past few years, has been exploring it by canoe and on his beloved 1970's Moto Guzzi motorcycles.

From time to time, he returns to the UK to 'get a breath of Britain' by hiking some of its many long-distance footpaths and riding around visiting friends and relatives on Royal Enfields. Writing about his trips and sharing them with others doubles the pleasure. He is a regular contributor to 'RealClassic' magazine and frequently posts to on-line motorcycle forums.